War and Innocence

A Young Girl's Life
in Occupied Norway (1940-1945)

Hanna Aasvik Helmersen

D1445787

HARA
PUBLISHING GROUP

Published by
Hara Publishing
P.O. Box 19732
Seattle, WA 98109
(425) 775-7868

ISBN: 1-883697-97-2
Library of Congress Number: 99-098075

Manufactured in the United States
10 9 8 7 6 5 4 3 2

Editor: Lynn Moen
Cover Painting: Aage Stein
Cover Design: Dennis "Ocean" Saisanith
Desktop Publishing: Lynn Moen
Map: Arne Moen

Contents

Dedication

To the memory of my beloved parents, who were both great and gifted storytellers. I have tried here to follow their lead.

Acknowledgments

I want to express my heartfelt gratitude:

To my long-time, faithful friend and mentor, Dennis K. Peters, who inspired me to start this project, and nurtured me to the end.

To my treasured husband, Hjaltar, who listened with patience and approval as chapter by chapter came to be.

To all my siblings, and especially to Ingebjørg, for sharing their memories.

To my son, Arne, whose love and computer expertise repeatedly rescued, supported and sustained me.

To my granddaughter, Jessica, who, when hearing my stories read, exclaimed, "Farmor, this should be in a library!"

To my friends, Dr. Lyle and Mildred Jensen, who read and liked the first, embryonic form of the manuscript.

To all the readers and reviewers who have added their knowledge, experience and input, to make up for what I lacked.

To my wonderful friend, Aage Stein, for creating such a gripping and emotionally correct cover painting.

And above all to my friend, my husband's cousin, Lynn Moen, who, more than anyone, helped turn the manuscript into a book. Her vision, knowledge, and great patience reassured me, time and again.

Preface

When my children were small they kept asking me, "Tell about when you were little. Tell about the war in Norway." After many years I decided to write these stories down for them. I wanted to describe a childhood vastly different from theirs. Others who read or heard these stories urged me to enlarge the manuscript to put the stories into context. They felt that it would be a valuable record of that time in Norwegian history, as experienced from the inside.

Source materials available to me in English had only short paragraphs here and there dealing with Norway's part in World War II. The Norwegian experience seemed to be just a footnote to history, but for those of us who experienced it firsthand it was something entirely different. It marked us for life.

The setting of this book is primarily Northern Norway, beyond the Arctic Circle. Into this remote region World War II literally arrived with a bang on April 9th, 1940. Life was drastically changed. Whole communities were uprooted and in flight. The sounds of war were everywhere. After Norway's capitulation to Germany two months later the country and its people suffered under an increasingly oppressive and brutal regime for five long years.

I have attempted to blend the personal stories with chapters containing my research to humanize the details of history and to transcend personal memories. I especially would like the younger generations to know and feel what it was like coming of age in a most difficult time, a time when horrible things took place. I wanted to show how, under harsh circumstances, ordinary people could lead both ordinary—and extraordinary—lives.

Hanna Aasvik Helmersen (October, 1999)

The Aasvik Family

Back: Torgunn (17), Odny (14); Front: Marit (18), Knut (11 months),
Hanna (9), Kirsten (6), Ingebjørg (20). Harstad, October 1940

Dagny Aasvik, "Mama"   Karsten Aasvik, "Papa"

1
When War Comes

She was my best friend. She was ten, I was eight. We were playing hopscotch in the front yard on a bare, dry piece of ground, surrounded by dirty, mushy left-over snow from the winter. The early April evening was mild and light, and we had hung our coats on the fence. The days were getting longer and longer. In another month there would be no night at all in this part of Northern Norway.

Suddenly Åse said: "The war will come soon."

A terrible feeling crept into my stomach. *Krig* is the Norwegian word for war and it had an ominous sound. I had heard of wars in Ethiopia and in Spain. One man from our community had gone to Spain to fight in the Civil War, and he did not come back. People were killed in wars. On my sister Torgunn's sixteenth birthday, September 3rd, 1939, England had declared war on Germany, and there was war in Poland, but that was so far away. It could not come here.

"Yes," said my friend, "it will."

The grown-ups had talked about the mines which had been laid in the fjord leading in to Narvik. The English had done that.

When we went to the grocery store, people's faces were somber. They spoke quietly, with much head shaking. The war will come soon, Åse had said. My stomach felt like it did when I had done something I

Hanna and Åse

1

wanted to hide from my mother, but now I hadn't. I still felt so very scared deep inside. The war will come soon.

Åse all of a sudden laughed. "Well, it is not going to come yet, because in two weeks Mama and I are going to Narvik to buy new shoes for me." I laughed too. I knew her logic was kind of silly, but somehow it comforted me.

Life was still the same, and it probably would always be. It was time to go inside and get ready for bed. We said good night to each other and she went across the highway and the field to her home.

It was early morning, very early, for it was still dark. Mama was bent over my bed, "You must get up and get dressed quickly. Something is going on and I don't know what it is, but we must be ready to leave if we have to."

Then I heard it. BOOM, BOOM far away. The sounds were all muffled, for it had started snowing and blowing outside. I rubbed my eyes, and started to remove my pajamas. "No," Mama said, "just keep them on underneath your other clothes." This was strange, but I always obeyed my mother.

I put on my sweater and the warm ski pants, heavy woolen socks, and my big sturdy winter boots. BOOM, BOOM, BOOM! The sounds were getting closer and closer. The house shook each time. Was this the war?

Mama said it was probably just testing. Up in the hills were some old guns which were used on our National Day, the 17th of May. But this was April 9th, so it was too early for that. BOOM, BOOM, BOOM! The windows rattled really hard and a lamp fell from the night stand and broke. Mama looked frightened. This scared me even more.

BOOM, BOOM, BOOM, BOOM! The big chandelier in the parlor crashed and two windows shattered. We screamed. Mama hushed us. My sister Odny, who was almost fourteen years old, had not finished dressing. She stood with her back supporting the bedroom door which had loosened from its hinges while she put on the rest of her clothes. There were a few more explosions, then silence.

Upstairs lived an old lady and her granddaughter Mary. We called the old lady Besta, a Norwegian word for grandmother. Besta knocked on the front door and they came into our big ranch-style kitchen. We were all there. Mama had left the blinds down. Now she secured them with heavy objects.

Besta had gotten some glass splinters inside her underpants and had cut herself on broken glass. Mama cleaned her cut while we all sort of snickered at the glass inside her underpants. How did it get there?

Mama decided Odny should go over to Åse's house to find out what was going on and what we ought to do. By now it was light outside, but the snow still kept coming, heavy and big flakes. The bare spot where we had played hopscotch the evening before was covered with over a foot of snow. The winter was still with us.

Åse's house (right), Hanna's house (left, to right of barn).
Narvik and its harbor (back).

After a while Odny came back, out of breath from running. "The war has come," she said. "The Germans have invaded Norway, and there are battles everywhere. Everyone is leaving. A big ship is burning not far from our house, and we must get out immediately, because they think the boilers are going to explode. They said we must come up to them, since they are farther away from the water."

I was glad to go to Åse's home. I always liked to play inside with her. We quickly put on our anoraks (parkas), scarves and mittens. Mama bundled up my baby brother Knut, who was just five months old, and put him in the big black buggy with the large wheels. The wheels couldn't move in the deep snow, so Torgunn and eighteen-year-old Marit, two of my older sisters, carried it. It was hard work. They had to lift their legs very high for each step.

I held my little sister Kirsten's hand and helped her. Mama took the big *spark* (Norwegian kick-sled), loaded it with bedding and some food and pushed it through the snow.

We could see the ship lying on its side, burning, with flames shooting up, but it was still snowing hard, so everything was like a picture out of focus.

Many people were gathered at Åse's house, discussing what to do. I knew them all. The coffee pot was on the stove, and the grown-ups were served coffee and cookies. The children got cookies with milk. We knew we had to play quietly, because the situation was too serious for loud talking and laughing.

Åse had a *Lappe dukke* (a Same or Lapp doll), dressed in a white reindeer-skin outfit, with bright colored borders and ribbons. We played with her for a while. The older children got board games out. The front door was continually opening and closing, each time with a gust of cold air, as people came and left.

We learned that people were walking out towards the west, away from Narvik and our community, Ankenes, which was south of Narvik across the harbor. We could see them on the road, groups of people moving as if it were Sunday on their way to church, except they were carrying things or dragging them on sleds or pushing *sparks.*

Mama did not know what to do as Papa was at work on the other side of Narvik. She did not want to leave without him, but he might not be able to get home. There was no ferry service on this day of war.

Åse's father stood by the window. It was no longer snowing, and he was looking at the mouth of the harbor. His chin and lips were trembling and his voice shook when he talked.

Again I felt that awful feeling in my stomach. When the grown-ups who made my world safe and normal were so frightened, what would become of us?

A big, dark warship came gliding into the harbor. Guns were sticking out from all sides. It looked like some giant insect monster invading our peaceful lives.The grown-ups decided we needed to get out of there at once. The rooms became noisy and full of commotion as we all put on our outerwear and got ready to leave.

We joined the rest of the community on the road and started to trudge westward through the snow. The country road had not been plowed, but hundreds of people, walking, pulling and pushing as many things from their homes as possible, had worn paths in the snow. We tried to step where the snow was trampled down.

Hanna's *spark.*

We walked and walked, almost two hours. My big sister Marit carried the baby buggy with a friend of hers. They got very tired. My sister Odny was sick with an earache. She got to ride on one of the *sparks.* I had my own little *spark,* but got tired and cold pushing it, so my sister Torgunn took turns with me and Mama. My youngest sister, Kirsten, whom we called Vesla (the little one), was put onto the back of a truck full of people. It moved slowly, but faster than we were walking. Soon we lost sight of it.

There was little talking. The cold wind stung our faces. My lips became so numb, I could not talk clearly. The same happened to the others. With stiff lips I asked my mother where we were going. She only shook her head and made a sign to me to just keep walking.

We moved out in the countryside beyond where I normally came. We passed the cemetery where my first baby brother was buried. It was off the road in a thin forest of fir trees. Today it was all white.

After a long time we came to Håvik to one of the biggest farms out in the country. Some of the people turned in there. Others had already stopped with family or friends, and others again kept walking. We did not have any family or friends out here, so we stopped at the big farm. They quickly gave us soup and bread. It felt so good to get warm again.

The grown-ups were talking. Each one had a bit of news. Some of it was contradictory. It was hard to know what was real and what was not. But the war was real.

My friend had been right. The war would come.

The war had come.

2
Strategic Narvik

Narvik, a small Norwegian town beyond the Arctic Circle, owed its existence to its ice-free harbor. High-grade Swedish iron ore could be shipped from there night and day throughout the year. In contrast, the Swedish shipping port of Lulea was closed by ice in winter for many months.

The ore came from the Gällivare mines in northern Sweden and was brought by railroad across the mountains and down to Narvik. This railroad track called Ofotbanen, built around the turn of the century and opened in 1902, runs through spectacular scenery—first across the mountain plateau, then clinging to the steep mountain-side through tunnels and over bridges with the Rombakfjord deep below.

In the years just before World War II, between seven and eight million tons annually were shipped from Narvik to countries all over the globe.

The harbor could accommodate many large iron ore ships waiting to be loaded. On April 8th, 1940, the day before the war started, twenty-five ships were anchored there. Sailors speaking many languages were a part of the daily city life, adding to Narvik's population of about ten thousand.

The biggest buyer of this iron ore was Germany. Germany had left the League of Nations in 1934 and was now engaged in rapid re-armament for which it needed ever-increasing amounts of steel.

Under the slogan *Ein Volk, Ein Reich, Ein Führer* (one people, one state, one leader), general military service was established. *Die Luftwaffe* (the air force) was built as well as thirty-six army divisions. More and more tanks and armored vehicles were rolling off the assembly lines, and the artillery which had been horse-drawn became increasingly motorized. The swastika became the national banner.

Soon Germany started to acquire more territory. In 1938 Hitler's army marched into Austria. This was called *Anschluss* (annexation), and meant that the German-speaking people were being connected to *Gross Deutschland* (Greater Germany). That was followed by the occupation of Czechoslovakia.

In May 1939 Finland, Sweden and Norway rejected a German invitation to sign a non-aggression pact. They did not feel threatened. In August the Soviet Union signed such a pact and Germany was allowed to establish and supply a base in North Russia: *Base Nord.*

However, on September 1st, Germany invaded Western Poland. Two days later Great Britain, France, India, Australia and New Zealand declared war on Germany. The Second World War had started.

Norway declared its neutrality. To prevent accidental, non-planned breaks of neutrality, the six army divisions were called in to active duty. Navy ships were disbursed along the coast. Small, old merchant ships were armed with guns and manned with navy personnel. The coastal fortresses were reactivated with reduced staff.

Soon news reached us that a Norwegian merchant ship had been torpedoed with the loss of seventeen sailors. September 17th saw the Russian invasion of Eastern Poland. Ten days later Poland capitulated.

On November 3rd, the day my baby brother was born, an American merchant ship, the *City of Flint,* was captured by German forces in the Atlantic. The ship arrived in Norway, contrary to the neutrality status. Norwegian marines entered and took the German sailors captive. The ship was returned to her American captain (who sailed for the USA). The Germans were kept at Kongsvinger Fortress, a bit southeast of Oslo.

On November 30th the Soviet Union attacked Finland with 600 thousand men. The Finnish army of 150 thousand men fought heroically, inflicting heavy losses on the Russians.

During this Finnish-Russian war, which we called The Winter War, the railroad from Narvik was used to supply the Finns. Mama and my sisters knitted socks and mittens with the index finger separate from the others. Mama said the soldiers needed to have them that way for shooting the guns. They had to be white, for the Finnish soldiers were dressed all in white so they could sneak up on the Russians without being detected.

Finnish refugees came on Ofotbanen to Narvik. Hearing foreign languages was not strange to us, but we were very intrigued by the Finnish children who had mastered both Swedish and Finnish. As we overcame our shyness we made friends, and soon learned many phrases and to count in Finnish.

The end of the Winter War was sad. Finland lost territory to Russia. Our newfound friends left, but we were also happy that the war and killings had ended there.

The news reached us that two British and one Greek merchant ship had been torpedoed by German submarines in Norwegian territorial waters. Great Britain claimed that Norway was not defending its neutral waters.

Britain was, of course, aware that Germany depended on the iron ore from Sweden for its war machinery. The British Admiralty studied how they could blockade this route, but the wheels moved slowly.

At that same time Hitler was planning to occupy Norway and Denmark to secure bases from where the Germans could control the Atlantic and the British fleet, as well as the Baltic.

The German occupation had been under consideration for a long time. An extensive espionage effort went on for years, especially in the mid to late 30's, with German "tourists," traveling salesmen, study groups, and film expeditions swarming over the country, getting to know and mapping every part—the coastline, military forts, strategic places and military readiness.

German U-boats were seen leaving Norwegian fjords and so-called "ghost planes" were seen flying above. They seemed especially interested in Narvik, Ofotbanen and the Swedish iron ore mines.

Even Hitler's yacht, *Grille,* arrived in Narvik harbor October 8th, 1936, with Germany's Minister of War, von Blomberg, his secretary and a large group of "friends" on board. They just "happened" to stop there for food and oil supplements. They also boarded an iron ore train to Abisko, Sweden, making good use of various types of cameras during the whole trip.

After Germany's invasion of Poland and the Allied declaration of war, the war action tapered off. In some international quarters some even called it "The Phony War."

But for the Norwegian merchant marine it was real enough. Between September 1st, 1939, and April 9th, 1940, fifty-eight Norwegian ships were sunk and 392 sailors perished.

Now we know that both the Allies and the Axis were preparing actions against Norway, although their motives were somewhat different.

The Allies' main concern was to stop the aggression of Germany and the Soviet Union, and to end the war.

The Germans wanted more *"Lebensraum"* (living space), more territories and power.

Both the Allies and the Axis were especially interested in the iron ore traffic through Narvik along the protected Norwegian coastal route down to the Continent.

The British wanted to blockade this traffic by mining Norwegian waters in order to force the iron ore ships out into the open Atlantic so they could break Germany at sea as they had done in World War I.

The Finnish-Russian war seemed like a good excuse to secure the port of Narvik while at the same time helping the Finns, but the war ended before any action was taken.

Still Churchill pressed for the invasion. The British Admiralty took its time, but they finally decided that the Norwegian coastal waters were to be mined April 5th, followed by a joint French-British landing in four places, if the Norwegians remained passive and gave in to diplomatic pressure or if the Germans made signs to invade Norway. After three days of delay the mines were laid on April 8. Two battalions of Allied forces boarded British warships in Scotland April 6th and 7th.

Hitler wanted the iron ore, of course, but also marine and air bases in Denmark and Norway to control the Baltic and the Atlantic. On January 13th, 1940, he started the invasion plans, at first called *"Studie Nord,"* which on January 27th became organized under the secret code *"Weserübung"* (Weser execise, named after the Weser river at Bremerhaven, from which the fleet sailed.)

Vidkun Quisling, founder of the Norwegian Nazi party, had traveled to Germany many times. He finally succeeded in seeing Hitler. He told him that Germany had many sympathizers in the Norwegian military. He impressed Hitler by outlining a scheme of takeover similar to the Austrian *Anschluss* (annexation).

On February 16th a German ship, the *Altmark,* was chased into a Norwegian fjord by the British destroyer *Cossack.* They believed the ship had British prisoners of war on board. They were correct and the prisoners were rescued.

Norway protested this breach of neutrality, but Quisling claimed that the *Cossack* episode had been planned by Britain and Norway to facilitate the Allies' occupation of Norway. This was enough for Hitler, who sent for General Nikolaus von Falkenhorst and ordered him to command and execute the invasion of Denmark and Norway on April 9th, 1940.

On April 8th, 1940, London and Paris proclaimed that they had mined the area south of Narvik. They did not know the Nazi invasion had already started. The Germans used merchant vessels to bring arms, ammunition and even horses into Norwegian harbors. The German fleet was inside the fjords, ready to strike, which they did early in the morning of April 9th, 1940.

The Second World War had arrived in Norway.

3
Occupation, April 9th, 1940

Late on April 8th the British Admiralty announced through the Norwegian Legation in London that German battleships and troop transport ships had been observed heading north off the Norwegian coast. They were assumed to be on their way to Narvik, and could arrive in the evening that same day.

By seven p.m. the new and costly British battleship, the *Renown,* with eight destroyers which had been engaged in laying mines, were ordered to keep the Germans out of Narvik.

The weather was terrible, with a storm from the Northwest Atlantic creating rough seas. It was also snowing hard and the visibility was extremely poor. Because of this, the British did not get underway till about three in the morning of April 9th.

About the same time, two Norwegian coast guard ships sighted nine warships in a line heading towards Narvik in the Ofotfjord at full speed. The snowstorm made it difficult to see their nationality.

Norway had feared that the British would attack the German ore ships in the harbor after operation Wilfred, the code name for mining the Norwegian fjords.

The Norwegian foreign minister (or secretary of state) had ordered that any attack on Narvik should be met by force. (That order was later amended to read: No attack on British ships, only German.)

In Narvik harbor the Norwegian defense prepared for battle, although they did not yet know whether it was against the British or the Germans. The Norwegian Narvik defense consisted of two old ironclad, coal-fired battleships, built in England in 1899, the *Eidsvold* and the *Norge.* They also had two submarines and three coast guard ships. The *Eidsvold* left the harbor and took up position just outside

The *Eidsvold* and the *Norge,* Norway's old iron-clads from 1899.

the entrance. The submarines were deployed to a safer harbor, further out in the fjord. The three coast guard ships were also dispatched to posts in the fjord. This is where they sighted the nine foreign warships, but they still did not know their nationality.

The ships were German. They were part of Fighting Group 1, destined for Narvik. Group 1 consisted of two battleships: the *Scharnhorst* and the *Gneisenau,* ten destroyers, and supply ships, some of which had already arrived pretending to be merchant vessels. Other ships arrived later.

In order to distract and mislead the British, the battleships did not enter Vestfjord, but veered off towards the northwest, sailing outside the Lofoten Islands. Around four a.m. the British and German ships sighted each other. The *Renown* fired with all twenty-six guns. The British destroyers also fired. The *Gneisenau* was hit, and its fighting power severely damaged. The *Scharnhorst* was not hit. These two increased their speed, escaped, and later returned to Germany. The *Renown* was also hit, but not seriously damaged. The British destroyers set off for Narvik.

On their way in to Narvik, Fighting Group 1 split up. Three German destroyers stopped to set off troops at what was supposed to be an armed Norwegian fort. They had planned to use this fort to defend against the British. To their dismay they found that the fort had not even been built. Three other destroyers went into Herjangsfjord to land troops which would take the Norwegian army training base Elvegårdsmoen.

The flagship *Wilhelm Heidkamp,* accompanied by two destroyers, headed directly for Narvik harbor. The tenth destroyer had been delayed far out in the fjord because of some problem.

At 4:15 the three ships were seen by the *Eidsvold.* It signaled them to stop, using lamp and Morse code. The signal was ignored, and the *Eidsvold* fired a warning shot. Our house was close to the shoreline and it was this first shot that had awakened my mother. She looked out but could see nothing through the heavy snowstorm and the dim, very early morning light.

The *Wilhelm Heidkamp* stopped and signaled that an officer would board. The ships were now about two hundred feet apart. A small boat brought a German officer who announced that the ships had only friendly intentions, namely to protect against British attacks, and that they expected Norwegian cooperation.

The *Norge's* commander was head of the Narvik defense group. His name was Askim. As soon as the German officer left the *Eidsvold,* her commander, Willoch, called Askim to confer with him about what to do. He in turn called the Norwegian Admiralty in Oslo. The order came back to fight.

Commander Willoch called the German officer, getting into his small boat, to inform him that the German force would be met with force. The two officers saluted each other and the German left. As he stepped into the little boat a red flare was fired. This was the signal the Germans waited for. Before the old Norwegian ironclad could get ready to fire, it was hit by three German torpedoes. They ripped open the whole side of the ship, and in twelve seconds the ship went down at 4:37 a.m. Commander Willoch together with 175 men perished. Only eight were saved.

The *Norge,* the other ironclad, had moved away from the pier where it had been anchored to maintain telephone contact. At 4:20 it sighted two destroyers. The snow was coming down so thickly that they disappeared from sight. Twenty minutes later they were seen again, entering the harbor. The *Norge* fired. The fire was returned. The first five torpedoes missed, but number six and seven hit. One minute later the *Norge* went down with 120 men. Ninety were rescued.

These were the explosions that shook our house that fateful morning. Mama told us later that she had heard cries coming from the water. The young Norwegian sailors had cried: "Mama, mama."

The explosions also abruptly awakened crews on the twenty-five merchant ships at anchor in the harbor. Most of the men thought it was a British raid. A German iron ore ship, the *Bockenheim* was fully loaded and ready for departure. It pulled anchor, and set off for the fjord at full speed. But it ran aground and started burning. This burning ship forced us to leave our home.

German soldiers boarded all the merchant ships—British, Dutch, and Swedish—and no ship was allowed to leave the harbor. Even while the torpedoes were sinking the old ironclads, the German mountain troops went ashore in Narvik. At five a.m. Narvik was occupied.

That same morning German forces invaded Denmark and four other Norwegian ports. It was the first major operation of the German Navy which would spearhead the invasion with five different groups, targeting five important Norwegian ports.

The German forces consisted of:
• Two Army Corps (two mountain divisions and seven infantry divisions).
• One Air Force Corps (290 bombers, 40 Stukas, 100 fighters, 500 transport planes, 70 float planes).
• Every warship in their fleet. Also forty-one troop and weapon

transport ships. Some of these were merchant ships, sent early from Germany so that they would arrive in the evening of April 8th in the Norwegian ports, too late to be searched till the next day by customs agents.

Four hours after the first German tanks rolled across the Danish border, the country capitulated and the swastika flew over Copenhagen.

In Norway the invasion met with resistance. Already before the Germans landed, Allied submarines attacked the transport ships and twenty-one German ships with many hundreds of men lost. During the first hours of April 9th five more ships were torpedoed, including the *Blücher,* the German Navy's newest and largest vessel, and the flagship for the Oslo invasion group.

But in spite of the first resistance, by 5:30 p.m. on April 9th, 1940, 10 thousand German soldiers had gone ashore in Norway, and instead of the Norwegian flag, the swastika was flying from official buildings.

At 5:27 p.m. Gross Admiral Raeder in Germany received this message:

OCCUPATION OF NARVIK, TRONDHEIM, BERGEN, STAVANGER, KRISTIANSAND, AND ARENDAL COMPLETED. OCCUPATION OF OSLO PROGRESSING. SOUTH OF OSLO SOME RESISTANCE FROM COASTAL FORTS. THE NORWEGIAN GOVERNMENT HAS LEFT OSLO.

4

At the Big Farm

When we arrived at the big farm, we expected to find my little sister, but she was not there. We asked the people we saw and those arriving after us if they knew where the truck had gone. Some said it had continued to a valley far away between the mountains. Others said it had gone to the end of the road where a ferry crossed a fjord arm.

Mama became distraught. "Lord God," she said, "we have to find Vesla." Vesla (the little one), was our pet name for Kirsten, the youngest of us six girls, and only five years old.

Although telephones were scarce, the big farm had one, so they started calling around to other farms. Nobody had seen the truck, or knew where it had gone. Mama was getting frantic. People tried to comfort her and calm her down. "Of course she will be found. Sooner or later someone will know." They were right. It wasn't too long before we learned where the truck was. We had actually passed that farm when we walked westward.

Marit walked back to get her, and in about an hour we could see her and Vesla coming on the road. Mama went out to meet them. We saw her bend down and hug my little sister and touch her face.

Vesla's face was swollen and dirty. She had been crying a lot, and had been so scared that we would never come to get her, and she would be alone forever and ever. Even after she had been found she would suddenly take a hard, fast breath, as if she were still crying, but she wasn't.

Evening came and we needed to sleep, but where? Many families were gathered in the farmhouse by now, probably thirty to forty people. There were old ones and parents, young men and women, and many children. My baby brother was the youngest.

We fell asleep everywhere, on sofas and in chairs, and even on the kitchen counter and dining table, but mostly on the floor. There were bodies all around, and funny sounds, moaning and purring and piping and whistling and gurgling and loud snoring. Once in a while someone would wake up and say something in a low voice, someone else would answer very softly, and then it would be quiet again, except for all the different sleeping noises.

I do not know how long I slept, but suddenly I became aware of people talking excitedly around me. Then I heard it. The shooting had started again.

This farm was quite a way from the fjord, with fields and the main road in between, but we could see the water. Out there in the gray light several warships were firing their big cannons. We could see the brief flare, then a few seconds later we heard the booming sound.

One of the young men was a high school student, and he said, "We know that sound travels about 300 meters per second. By counting the seconds between the flare and the sound we can tell how far away they are." So we counted the seconds and figured the distance. Then someone said that even if they did not shoot directly at the farm we could be hit by metal fragments called shrapnel. We needed to go down in the cellar which had been dug under the house.

In those days most older homes had entrances to the root cellar both from the outside and from the inside through an opening in the kitchen floor. It was covered by a hinged door in the floor, and usually hidden by a woven runner. When the weather was really stormy, or the outside entrance was covered with deep snow it was better to use the floor entrance.

As they opened the hinged door an earthy smell spread out in the kitchen. The stairs were steep and narrow, like a ladder, and we had to back down, one at a time. It was dark down there. Hanging from the rough wooden ceiling was a light bulb on a wire. It gave very little light, but after a few minutes we could see better.

Around the walls were bins for sacks of potatoes and other root vegetables. They had been full in September, but were now nearly empty. There were also barrels with salted fish and meat. The floor was hard-packed earth.

Each person tried to find some place to sit—on boards or barrels or boxes. Some stepped into the bins and sat on the vegetable or potato sacks. Empty sacks were spread on the floor for us children. The cold from the floor crept through the sacks and made our bottoms icy, so we wiggled and moved as much as we could, and sometimes just stood up.

An old man named Hans Persa sat down on a full potato sack. Then we heard a muffled voice from the bin, "You're sitting on my head, Hans Persa."

"Heh?" said the old man.

"Hans Persa, you are sitting on my head!"

But the old man could not hear very well, so his wife Susanna shouted, "You can't sit there! Move!"

"I sit good, I sit good," said Hans Persa.

"Yes, but you are sitting on Askheim's head."

Hans Persa slowly got up on his legs, turned his whole body around and peered into the bin. "Oh, is it you?" he said calmly.

Everyone started laughing. It was the first laughter we had heard in many hours.

We could faintly hear other sounds from the outside. Explosions. Every so often there were little knocks on the stone walls high up. Then the grown-ups would look at each other with meaningful looks.

A woman with a good voice started singing Luther's hymn *A Mighty Fortress Is Our God.* Others joined in. We all knew many verses by heart. In the Norwegian schools and for confirmation children had to memorize lots of hymns, even those with fourteen, sixteen verses, and we did not find that difficult. My mother always sang while she worked in the house, hymns and songs about nature. Outdoors we played many song games, so singing was a very important part of my childhood.

I really liked Luther's hymn. It made me feel twice as safe—safe because we were sitting deep down under ground behind thick stone walls, like a real fortress, and also because God was a mighty fortress for us.

We sat in the cellar till there were no more explosions for a while. Then we climbed up, one by one. How light and bright the world above looked.

Later we learned that an important sea battle had been fought that night or early morning. Outside the cellar walls we found metal fragments along the ground, and there were fresh chips in the rocks. But we had all been kept safe in our fortress.

My oldest sister Ingebjørg was nineteen, almost twenty, and was work-ing as a nurses' aide in the hospital in Narvik. Mama worried a lot about her safety. People said: "Even in a war hospitals are safe. Bombs and guns are not aimed at hospitals, so your daughter is as safe or probably safer than anyone." This helped us feel better about her.

But Papa was still absent. Mama told us that even if he was able to get away from work and cross the harbor he might not be able to find us. That was a big problem.

However, the day after the war started, suddenly he was there, with us. He had been given permission to leave for one day, but he had to return, otherwise he might be executed if found. Papa told us about all the destruction he had seen—houses burning, soldiers everywhere, people fleeing, the harbor full of sunken ships with just the masts and smoke-stacks sticking up above the water. He had gotten a friend with a motor boat to take him across the harbor, and then he had walked for two hours to get to us after he found out where we were.

He and my mother discussed what to do now. Mama did not think he needed to go back. This was wartime and normal rules did not apply. But Papa said that first of all, he had given his word of honor, and secondly, if he were found disobeying orders he would be shot. So he had to return.

Mama cried. Papa held her and hugged her and said he would return as soon as he could, and he hoped it would be very soon. He had found our house still standing, and had brought some more bread and jam with him.

After eating, he dressed and started walking back. But first he hugged and kissed each of us, stroked our hair and asked us to be good and brave, to help Mama and be obedient to her. We said we would.

Mama walked with him a short distance. They hugged for a long time, then separated.

Papa kept turning around, waving. He waved and waved until we couldn't see him any more. Mama kept crying. I couldn't remember Mama crying before.

War was a terrible thing.

Oluf Larsen's house on the big farm.

5
The First Battle of Narvik

The German occupation of Narvik had cost them dearly. Underway the storm had washed many of the crew overboard, but the destroyers steamed on with no attempt to rescue them. The *Norge,* before it went down, had also been able to damage some German destroyers, which led to many wounded. The hospital was full of dying and wounded. Most were Norwegians, but there also were many German soldiers.

The Occupation Forces immediately took over the official buildings, and set up several air defense batteries and automatic weapons posts. General Dietl was in charge of the land-based soldiers, and Commander Bonte on the flagship *Heidkamp,* was responsible for the navy.

When evening came April 9th, the Germans were uneasy. First of all, they knew that the British were in the Vestfjord. Secondly, their artillery had not arrived. Two of the supply ships had been sunk and the third went to Bergen to avoid the British. Most importantly there was little oil. Only the tank ship *Jan Wellem,* which had arrived from *Base Nord* in Russia, made it to Narvik. Consequently the original plan of refueling and returning all the destroyers to Germany immediately after the occupation was no longer possible.

It was almost evening of April 9th before the English knew and accepted what had happened, especially that the Germans had come as far north as Narvik. Finally Captain Warburton Lee on the destroyer *Hardy,* which had been part of the mine-laying expedition, was given permission to attack. He had learned that there were six German destroyers and several German transport ships in Narvik harbor. He decided to attack "at dawn and high tide," to minimize the danger the mines posed, and to maximize the element of surprise. With the *Hardy* were the destroyers *Hunter, Havoc, Hostile* and *Hotspur.*

The weather was miserable—foggy and snowy like the day before, with heavy winds from the northwest, and poor visibility. The German *Dieter von Roeder* was guarding the harbor entrance, but went in to refuel, anchoring at 4:25 a.m. on April 10th.

Just then the British arrived. First they fired their front cannons, then made a quarter-turn and let loose the torpedoes from their broadside; now another quarter-turn and the stern cannons went into action. They repeated this twice. At 4:35 the alarm went off on the German ships. By then the harbor was a living hell. Two of the destroyers were refueling, one on either side of the *Jan Wellem*. This was normally a six-to-seven hour operation per ship. Behind these three ships was the *Anton Schmidt*. It was hit mid-ship and broke in two. The front half sank, and the back half tipped onto the destroyer in front so it could not move. The water quickly became covered with oil, and started to burn. Only a few of the sailors were rescued from this inferno.

On the flagship *Wilhelm Heidkamp*, Commodore Bonte and his staff ran up onto the command deck. Then a torpedo hit the stern. The ammunition magazine exploded, flew up in the air, and landed on the front deck. Several projectiles hit the command bridge. Commodore Bonte and most of the officers were killed. The *Wilhelm Heidkamp* eventually sank. The *Dieter von Roeder* was hit and started burning. The *Hans Ludemann* and the *Hermann Kunne* were also damaged. Many of the iron ore ships were hit, burned and sank.

In order to maneuver better, the British moved away from the harbor entrance and out into the wider fjord. Gliding out from Herjangsfjord came the three German destroyers; *Erich Köller, Erich Giese,* and *Wolfgang Zenker.* The British moved even further out. From another fjord came two more German destroyers, the *Georg Thiele* and the *Berndt von Arngrim.* They all concentrated on the British flagship Hardy. Its command bridge was hit, and all the men there were either killed or wounded. Another officer dragged himself up to the steering wheel and tried to navigate, but then the engine got a direct hit. The ship went aground. Some of the British sailors swam ashore, bringing with them the seriously wounded, including the captain, Warburton Lee. He died before they reached shore. About 170 half-naked, half-frozen sailors were able to reach land. Here the Norwegian civilians took them in and helped them in every way. The wounded were brought to a small hospital in Ballangen, a community west of Narvik.

The *Hunter* was torpedoed and sank. Some of the survivors became German POWs, (prisoners of war) but forty-three escaped capture. The *Hotspur* was severely damaged, but remained afloat. The *Hostile* was lightly damaged, The *Havoc* not at all. With the *Hotspur* in tow, these three ships escaped. On their way out they met the German supply ship *Ravensfeld,* loaded with cannons and ammunition for Narvik. It was boarded and sunk.

Narvik suffered a great deal of damage. Merchant ships, piers and buildings were destroyed. In Ankenes, my home community, our white, octagonal church received a direct hit, but did not burn. Narvik Hospital, where our sister Ingebjørg worked, received even more dead and wounded. The rooms, corridors and stairways were packed.

Finally that sea battle we saw from the farm windows and hid from in the root cellar that early morning, April 10th, 1940, was ended.

Ankenes Cemetery. The front stone reads:
"A Sailor of the Second World War
Royal Navy HMS *Hardy* 10 April 1940"

6

Refugees

The owners of the big farm, the Oluf Larsen family, were very good to us. They shared their food with all these crowding strangers, almost as if we were family, and never let us understand how inconvenient it was for them to be invaded by so many.

But it soon became evident that we could not stay there longer. All the time we heard different kinds of explosions.

My next oldest sister Marit tried to get back to our house to gather some more clothes and food, but she was stopped by some men in the forest between the farm country and the town. She said they were English sailors who had escaped their sinking ships. Marit had taken evening classes in English and could speak a little with them. The sailors told her she could not go back to Narvik because the Germans were there.

It was hard for me to keep all these stories straight. But I understood that my life was totally disrupted, and I had no idea what the next day would be like. This was war.

Horses were brought out and hitched to a couple of wagons, for the old people to sit on. The children and younger folks walked behind. We were heading further west to the end of the road where a ferry would pick us up and bring us to an isolated community far away between the mountains. They thought we would be safer there.

We had to leave our dog behind. His name was Bob, and he was golden brown. When he was a puppy he had fallen into the engine room where Papa worked, and had broken his leg. It healed crooked, so he walked and ran with a funny limp.

I also had to leave my little *spark* behind. Papa had carved my name on it, and it was very special to me. He had given it to me when I started first grade. Mama said that when the war was over we would come back and pick up both Bob and the spark. I felt very sad when we left.

It was evening when we arrived at the end of the road. We had to wait quite a while before the ferry-people came, but finally we were on board. We went down into the passenger lounge. It was broad at one end and narrow at the other. Along the walls were long, curved, leather covered benches, and in the middle were two benches with their backs touching. The room smelled of machine oil, and urine because the toilet was close by. It was the kind we flushed by pumping sea water into it after using it. We were not used to this kind. At home, like most people then, we had an outhouse with a wooden seat with two openings, one for grown-ups and one for children.

The engines went donk-donk-donk-donk in the quiet late winter evening. It was not really dark, just a kind of gray light. We passed small communities I had heard of by name, but never visited before. No life was to be seen.

About 2 o'clock in the morning we arrived at the very end of the fjord called Skjomen, and the place itself was Elvegård. We marched up to some long, low buildings called the English cabins. This area was well known for its rivers and waterfalls, and in the summers many English tourists would come to fish for trout. The cabins had been built for them.

We entered a long, rustic dining hall with endless tables, kitchen counters, a big wooden stove and metal sink. Through the door we could see rooms with bunk beds.

We were all tired and hungry, and after a while some farm ladies came and started a fire in the stove. Then they got out huge kettles and made oatmeal porridge. I was not terribly fond of this porridge, but anything tasted OK. We got a little sugar to sprinkle on top, and milk in heavy, white mugs to drink with it. Soon the benches around the tables filled with people.

I listened to them talking. They called us refugees. In Norwegian the word is *flyktning* or people who flee. There was a lot of discussion about us. What would they do with all these refugees?

Soon some of the leaders of the community arrived. They decided we would be housed with different families.

Our family was sent to stay with the woman who used to be the community midwife. She and her husband had a big house with a large, extra bedroom with three beds. It was big enough for six people and the baby.

Finally at five or six in the morning we were put to bed. It was so weird, but everything was weird. We were no longer families and neighbors and friends like we used to be.

We were refugees. Life had been turned upside down, and nothing was normal any more.

7

Troubles At the Midwife's

The midwife, Mrs. Olsen, was old and forgetful. Her husband was even older, a gray little man who did everything his wife told him. She had a large bosom and was kind of broad all over. She always wore a knitted woolen pullover which had once been white. Her voice was gruff, and her words were short and sharp, almost like a dog bark.

They had a foster daughter living with them. Her name was Harriet and she was retarded. Her head was smaller than normal, and she always wore a grey-striped knitted hat with a long tassel on top. Harriet was supposed to help in the house, but she was clumsy, and her foster mother was forever barking at her: "Har-r-r-iet!" The Rs were loud and angry.

We tried to stay outdoors as much as possible so we wouldn't be in anybody's way, or make anybody mad. The weather was getting milder. The snow was melting fast, making little rivers everywhere, and our shoes muddy. We always took our big shoes off before walking into the house. Mrs. Olsen liked that. Harriet stomped in and out with long, brown rubber boots on.

All the time we could hear the sounds of war from behind the tall mountains. It was like thunder, sometimes loud and close by, other times more muffled and farther away, but almost constantly there. Mama was very worried about Ingebjørg and Papa. The neighbors looked at us with great sympathy in their faces. We did not know it, but some of them had heard that my father's dead body had been seen in one of the streets in Narvik. Mama started to get dizzy spells. She had to lean on one of my older sisters when walking outside.

One of the neighbors there was Swedish born. When the Olsen cows went dry we got milk from the Lindström farm. One day in her despair

Mama exclaimed: "Oh, I wish Hitler and all his men were dead!" Mrs Lindstrom answered very softly: "Yes, or that they would have a change of heart." (In Swedish, *"Ja, eller at dom ville fatta et annat sinn."* or: Yes, or that they would get to a different mindset.)

My mother was amazed at those words. She told us about that, and reflected with us about the consequences of how we think, how it will affect our lives and actions.

More and more war planes flew over the valley. We could see their markings under their wings and tell if they were German or Allied. The German planes had black crosses outlined in white. The Allied had white circles, sometimes with blue inside. Within a few minutes of their disappearance behind the mountain, we would hear the thunder start again.

On the farm the food was similar to what we were used to. We had bread with margarine, cheese or jam, and milk to drink for the morning meal. In the middle of the day we had dinner, usually fish and potatoes. In the evening bread and milk again, or porridge.

But since they had a little farm they had home-made sausages and salted, dried meat as well. The sausages were long, thin, hard and gray. When they were sliced the meat inside was brownish-black. I didn't like them very much, especially if Mrs. Olsen fried them, and dumped them with all the yellow fat on my plate. But I tried to be good and not make trouble. Mama said we had to be thankful that we had a place to stay, and food to eat.

My favorite food was bread with margarine and red currant jam. I also liked to just break bread into a bowl, and pour milk over it.

Mr. Olsen came back from the country store one day and said they were running out of food. There was no more margarine, and no yeast for bread making. "Well, then we have to make sour dough," said Mrs. Olsen. I don't know what happened, but the loaves of bread turned flat and small and hard, and they tasted sour. She did not like them either.

One day she made a big batch of dough in a large wooden trough. She made little balls which she clapped flat and baked on top of the wood stove. They were called *klappakaker* and they tasted good, especially with a special kind of cheese called *gomme*. It was soft and brown and sweet, and could be spread on the breadcakes. She made several stacks of these, and covered them up with a kitchen towel, then went to bed.

The next morning when she came down into the kitchen she looked at all this bread, then at Mama and said, "Did you make all of these?"

Mama replied, "No dear Mrs. Olsen, you made them yourself last night." No, she could not remember that at all. Mama made a sign with her eyes that we should not laugh or say anything.

Another evening her husband took the rowboat out to fish. He came back after we had gone to bed. The nights were almost completely light now. He must have been hungry, for he had cooked some fish and eaten.

The next morning when she came down she noticed some spills on the table, fish bones and skin. She pulled her woolen vest off, wiped the table with it, saying, "How could you leave all this mess? Don't you know I am a hater of dirt?" Then she put her vest on again. We were shocked, but Mama just made her sign to us not to say anything.

Mama was in the rocking chair nursing my baby brother. Suddenly she noticed something crawling across his head. "Oh God," she said, "There is a louse crawling on the baby's head." She looked more closely, and found several more. We were all inspected, and sure enough, we were full of lice.

Mrs. Olsen was very matter-of-fact about it. She told Mama that everyone had lice nests on their bodies, and two kinds of lice, brown head lice and white body lice with an ace of spades on their backs.

Mama was in tears. We had only the clothes we were wearing and had worn for two weeks now. How could she get rid of the lice?

She washed our underwear and pajamas, and hung everything on lines in the kitchen to dry. Then she got hold of a special kind of vinegar which she worked into our hair. We also had to use a special comb with very fine teeth which was supposed to pick up any lice or eggs. But all her efforts were in vain. We still had lice.

Mama talked with some other refugees, and they decided it would be best if we could get away from this place as soon as possible. The food situation was becoming very difficult as well.

Then my baby brother got sick. He was feverish and coughing and crying. No clinic or doctor or medicines were available in this community at the end of a long fjord between the mountains.

Mama had already lost 3 babies, a set of twins before I was born, and my first baby brother when I was two years old. Now she feared for our new brother. He was so special, the only boy among six girls, and the last to arrive.

I remembered some things about my first little brother. I used to sit by his buggy or cradle and sing to him, because he was sick his whole, short life of five months. There was one special song I sang, and even today when I hear or sing it I want to cry. It was *"Milde Jesus, du som sagde At til dig skal barna gå."* (Gentle Jesus, you who said that to you shall children come.)

I remember the doctor coming to see him, and I sat on Papa's lap by the door. I had to be very still, and not ask any questions because the doctor was a very important man and must not be disturbed. Mama spent so much time with this baby in the hospital. One of her friends, who was from Denmark, looked after us. She spoke funny and had big, yellow teeth. She was nice, but I was still scared of her and wanted my Mama.

My first baby brother died in November. They would not let me go to the funeral or cemetery. I had to stay at home. I sat at the kitchen table by the window and looked at the snow falling. If I looked just at the snow I felt like I was floating up into the sky. They told me my baby brother was now an angel in heaven, and that he would look after me always. As I kept floating upwards looking at the snow, I expected to see my baby brother any minute, right outside my window, waving to me. I sat there for a long time, but I never saw him, and I felt sad. For many years he was an unseen presence in my life.

And now our second and only baby brother was so sick, so very sick. Mama wanted him baptized in case something should happen to him also. If he were baptized, his soul would be safe with God, even if he died. But no pastor was available. She contacted the deacon of the church and arranged for him to perform a home baptism. Mrs. Olsen would be the godmother, and hold the baby during the ceremony.

They filled a wash bowl with warm water. The deacon was given a white towel to hang on his forearm. He read from the Hymnal all the words for infant baptisms which the pastor usually read. I knew most of them by heart.

Then they came to the place where he asked: What is the child's name? Mrs. Olsen had already asked Mama many times before the ceremony what his name was. But she could not remember, so Mama said each name, one at a time, and Mrs. Olsen repeated them, "Knut Jack Arild." The deacon took a handful of water three times and sort of washed the top of my brother's head while he said: "Knut Jack Arild Aasvik, I now baptize you in the name of the Father and the Son and the Holy Spirit, Amen."

Then he wiped him with the white towel. My brother did not say anything. He just looked at the deacon with his big, blue eyes. In the church the children usually screamed during this ceremony, but here it was very quiet. We knew this was a very sacred time. My baby brother was now safe with God no matter what happened.

Luckily he started getting well almost right away, and we wondered if the special presence of Jesus had made a miracle come to pass. We were very happy, because we loved our only brother very much.

8
Ingebjørg and a Time for Courage

Our oldest sister Ingebjørg, who was 19, together with another girl rented a room in a private home in Narvik, close to the hospital where they worked.

On the morning of April 9th they didn't know about the battle in the harbor and on the fjord. As they started walking to the hospital, two soldiers jumped up from a ditch and pointed their rifles at them. They were, of course, terribly frightened, and even more so when they realized these were German. Somehow, by gesturing and pointing to the hospital on top of the hill, and showing the nurses' uniforms they were wearing under the coats, they were allowed to continue.

At the hospital the wounded, dying, and dead were already being brought in. Soon the beds and gurneys were full. The sight was dreadful. They had never cared for injuries like these in peacetime. Those rescued from the oil-covered, flaming sea had gruesome burns and were screaming in agony. Others had body parts missing, body cavity ripped open, gaping flesh wounds with bones sticking out, and blood, blood, blood everywhere.

More and more kept arriving. Some were carried, some were pulled on sleds. One man with both legs missing from the knees down was brought in a rocking chair carried on the shoulders of two men. There he sat up in the air with the tattered pant legs and pieces of bloody skin dangling down from the seat.

The hospital staff worked frantically to stop the bleeding, clean and bandage the wounds, re-align the broken bones, give pain medication, sterilize needles and other equipment. This was before the days of disposables and modern sterilizing techniques, so everything had to be washed and boiled. They worked all day and all night. No time for food or sleep. My sister said the whole thing was totally unreal.

After a while she no longer heard the screams or reacted to the horror. She just continued her daunting and ghastly tasks.

After the Germans took over the city early in the morning, they met with the mayor and the city council. It was important for the occupation forces not to be bogged down with civilian administration, at first. One of the agreements they made was for the Germans to establish their own *Lazarett*, that is, a medical facility for the German wounded. They realized that the Community Hospital could not function in the present state of overflow.

In spite of this, the demands on the hospital staff were unrelenting. The sea battle on April 10th brought in more wounded and dead. Then on April 13th the British fleet came back in full force to finish off the German naval forces left there. The rest of the German destroyers were sunk. British planes bombed the harbor and city. The sounds of explosions volleyed back and forth between the mountains. It was a deafening inferno of noise, fire and smoke.

When it was over, large portions of Narvik lay in ruins. Also, on the Ankenes side of the harbor, many homes burned down, including our own. The harbor had become a graveyard for over 30 ships, partly or totally submerged. When the British battleship *Warspite* and her escorting destroyers steamed out of Narvik, they could report that all effective German naval strength in Narvik had been crushed. The German Navy had been demolished to the point that it would never be able to play any role in the preparations that were going on for the German invasion of England.

On April 9th part of the Narvik defense force became trapped inside the school building where they had sought refuge. What should they do? To fight two thousand or more German soldiers was pure insanity for 209 men. But they felt that capitulation was not an option either. They decided to try to escape. In broad daylight they marched out of the school building, single file, rifles on their shoulders. One of their leaders was Major Omland. The streets were full of Germans armed to the teeth. The sight of the Norwegian soldiers caught them by surprise. They just stared. *Was ist los?* (What is happening?) The Norwegians smiled and waved. Some of the Germans waved back. A German guard stepped forward with rifle pointed and told the Major that they could not pass. Major Omland smiled and answered, *"Doch, wir marschieren. Guten Morgen!"* (Well, we are marching. Good morning!)

And so they did, single file across town, to the railroad station about twenty minutes away. From there they continued further, on the tracks up to the mountains, where they became part of the forces that carried on the war against the Germans for two more months. This daring escape was one of the deeds that boosted Norwegian morale during the dark days of occupation.

Narvik on fire (above left)

Narvik in ruins (above right)

The ship graveyard in Narvik harbor (left and below)

9

Seeking Refuge Again

We spent almost three weeks at Elvegård. Then food became very scarce, and finally someone arranged for a fishing boat to take us away. We were heading for another fjord further south. We had heard that the Norwegian army had dug in there, and that supplies of food were available.

The refugees crowded on board the small boat. We sat on the deck, for there was no passenger lounge, only a small cabin where the fishermen slept and made coffee. Again the boat went donk-donk-donk-donk, and in between the mountains, where the fjord became narrow, the sound echoed back at us.

I learned a new song on that trip. It was about a boy who returned to his childhood home after he had become a grown man, and found that the only thing remaining was the lilac tree. It reminded him of all the love he had received from his mother and father, all the pet names they had given him, the stories they had told, the songs they had sung for him.

It was such a sweet and sad song, and the lady who sang it had a pretty, clear soprano voice. She was the mother of Sylva, a girl I knew, who also had a lovely voice.

One winter evening before the war started, my best friend Åse and I had gone out to play with Sylva. We sat outside on an old cement foundation, dangling our legs, and sang and sang all the songs we knew. Above us the Northern Lights flamed across the sky, the stars glittered, and the moon made blue shadows in the snow. It was such a magic evening.

Before we started home we went inside Sylva's home to get warm. Her family was different in that they did not belong to the Lutheran

State Church, but were Freethinkers. They were so friendly, and also unconventional in many ways.

They were the only people I knew close to my home who had a *støvsuger,* a vacuum cleaner. It made a lot of noise and sucked up everything. Once Sylva's mom let me put my hand close to the nozzle, and it surprised and scared me, pulling on my hand.

Now we were refugees together on a ship. We sang lots of songs as we chugged along. Those who had brought food shared it with those who had none. We traveled for many hours.

Once a war-plane came flying low. I cannot remember whether this one had the German cross or the Allied circle on its wings, but I do remember people talking about bombs dropping, and we were scared.

Late in the evening we arrived at another small place. There was a pier, and a small store with a post office. There was also a little waiting room where the local people sat while they waited for the local steamship which carried people, goods and mail along the coast.

My brother had pooped his pants, and he was fretful. We went with Mama upstairs to the family who operated the store and post office and steamship trade. Mama asked if she could please have a little water to clean the baby. The lady was not very friendly, but she gave Mama some cold water in a basin, saying, "We had nothing to do with this, and we can't take care of all these people." Then she hoisted herself up on the kitchen counter, and sat there dangling her legs.

I could tell from Mama's face that she was angry, but she said in a calm voice, "We had nothing to do with this war either, but we have been forced from our homes, and have been homeless for three weeks. My children are tired and hungry. I hope that you will not have to go through the same, and on top of all be treated with such unfriendliness."

The lady did not say anything, but she jumped down from the counter, went into the back room, and came out with a plate of crackers which she passed around to us. The crackers were hard and dry, but when we chewed them a long time the bites got bigger inside our mouths, and that helped to take some of the hunger away.

At midnight a truck arrived and we clambered into it. The truck bed had a canvas cover like a domed tent, but the floor was bare. We had to sit on the floor. This time of the year the ground was thawing, which made the roads full of huge holes. What an uncomfortable ride that was! We tried to laugh about it every time the truck hit one of those holes, and we shook and bumped up and down.

Finally we arrived at Korsnes. It was a bigger community with a school-house and church, warehouses and even a small building provided for the district doctor to stay and use when he saw patients on his regular visits. We were placed there the next day.

But that first night we stayed with the family who ran the shipping agency. They were so kind to us. They gave us soup and bread in the middle of the night, and helped make us comfortable on the floor so we could sleep.

The next day was April 29th, my sister Odny's 14th birthday. It was a sad birthday with no cake and no gifts and no party. The war had ruined everything.

The family who ran the shipping agency was from Bergen in the southwestern part of Norway. They have a different dialect. They had a little daughter named Kaspara, and when they said her name the R sounded way down in the throat and not in the mouth as ours did. My little sister was fascinated by this, and it was not long before she too said Kaspar-r-ra with the gurgling R. We thought that was so funny.

All this moving around was irksome and not too much fun, but we saw and learned a lot of things we had not experienced in our quiet little community at home. The places we had only heard about before became real, with different sounds and smells and new faces.

We met other children who also were homeless, and who spoke other dialects than we did. One family had a chicken farm. I had never heard of a chicken farm before. Most people I knew had a few hens for laying eggs just for their own family. One girl had a father who was a military captain. Up to that time I only knew of sea captains. Life was somehow bigger than I had realized before the war started.

I don't remember many details of the next few weeks. The days seemed to float together into a few pictures. We stayed in the doctor's building on a pier that jutted out over the water.

Here I ate whale meat for the first time. It was dark red, almost black. Mama sliced it, sprinkled salt and pepper on, pounded the slices with the back of her cutting knife till they were almost flat to make them tender. She fried them with onions in a black skillet. I really liked the taste of it, although it was still quite chewy.

But first we had to get rid of the lice. Mama rubbed kerosene into our scalp, then wrapped our heads in towels or scarves overnight. The kerosene burned and hurt, but Mama said it would really kill the pesky vermin. It was so hard to sleep, and I woke up many times during the night with the burning and pain.

In the morning, when she removed the towel, she saw the back of my head was a big, oozing wound. Somehow it had not done that to my siblings, just me. I could tell from Mama's eyes that it was bad, and they would not let me look at it in the mirror. She decided we really needed to see a doctor, but there was none.

Then someone mentioned that the military had a doctor. We trudged off to the camp, a good distance away. My head hurt and itched, and I wanted to put my hands back there and scratch or do something, but I must not touch it.

A friendly soldier brought us to the tent where the doctor was. Mama told him the whole story. He looked at me, shook his head and said, "Poor child, this is not very comfortable for you." I nodded. He was certainly right about that.

He told Mama to boil water, let it cool, and rinse the wounds several times a day with this. I don't remember if we got any medicine to put on it, but he gave me some pills for the pain. He reassured Mama that she had done the best she could, and he was sure the lice were dead. In a short while scabs would form, and I would be OK again.

He also cut off as much hair as he could. I thought I must have looked like a freak.

Sleeping was still hard, because I could lie only on my stomach, with a rolled-up towel for a pillow next to my ear to take the pressure off the back of my head. In a few days it was much better but it took a long time before all the scabs fell off.

Mama also heated big kettles of water and washed all our clothes on a washboard. We walked around in funny, borrowed clothes that did not fit, until everything was dried and ironed. Then we felt wonderfully clean again.

The sun was getting warmer every day, and we knew that summer was coming.

10
Times for Celebration

Every day rumors about the war were flying. We heard about the Allies who were our friends as opposed to the Axis who were enemies. Some said our friends were winning; others said no, the Germans were marching forward. Mama worried about Papa and Ingebjørg, our oldest sister. We had heard nothing from them.

One day we were offered a better place to stay. A sea captain with whom Papa had sailed lived some distance away in a big house. Their grown daughter came walking to us and asked if we wanted to live upstairs with them. They had space, and cows so there would be milk. They also had potatoes and a rowboat for fishing on the fjord. It sounded good. In a few days we trudged off to this place some kilometers away.

We still had no possessions and no money. What we owned was the big, black baby buggy, some bedding, a bread box and two knives, and the clothes on our bodies.

When we arrived we were received well. Mrs. E. and my mother visited. Soon Mrs. E. started to ask questions. When she learned that Papa had not sailed with her husband for many years, that we did not know where he was right now, or even if he was alive, and that we had no money, her friendliness disappeared.

In the evening I heard my mother talking with my sisters about this. She said she thought Mrs. E. probably had planned to rent out the upstairs in order to make money. I don't know how they worked this out, but we remained there. There may have been some emergency funds available for refugees.

My sister Marit was good at knitting and sewing. At the country store she and Mama were able to buy fabric, so she started to make dresses for us. They also bought new underwear and tennis shoes.

The 17th of May is a big day in Norway. We call it many names: *Grunnlovsdagen* (Constitution Day), *Nasjonaldagen* (National Day), *Barnas Dag* (Children's Day). During normal times we would have parades and games and speeches. We would get special food, and Norwegian flags would fly everywhere. There would be music and singing and dancing. Usually we got new clothes, and carried small flags with balloons attached on top of the sticks. Next to Christmas Eve, it was the best day of the year.

But this year the flag poles were empty. There were no celebrations, no parades, no music. Norway was at war. Even children could feel the sadness of it all.

One good thing happened. We had new clothes. Oh, how wonderful that brand new cotton fabric smelled. Our dresses were stiff and clean with puffed sleeves and round collars, and buttons in front. The fabric had flowers printed all over. I felt beautiful this 17th of May, except for my hair which was still all chopped up.

When we went out to play, we had to be very careful so we wouldn't get dirty, and we could walk only where the road was dry. But we sang lots of songs and waved sticks, pretending they were flags, and we shouted: *"Hurra for Syttende Mai"* (Hurrah for the 17th of May!)

Marit had been visiting at the neighbor's farm. We saw her running home, fast. She was waving her arms up in the air as she ran, and looked very excited. We did not know what was wrong. She bounded upstairs, and we after her. We knew something extremely important had happened.

She was all out of breath. She said, "Papa." Then she had to take a breath. "There was a telephone call." Another breath. "Papa has been found, I mean he has found us, and he is coming."

We all spoke at once, "Where is he? When is he coming? How will he get here? Who told you?" She did not know all the answers. A neighbor got a phone call, and the connection was poor, but he thought Papa had said that he hoped to be here the 20th of May.

In three days we would see Papa again! It had been 40 days since he left. Oh, how happy we were. Mama said we must remember to say a special thank-you prayer tonight, and ask God to continue to watch over him and our sister.

This was a special 17th of May after all. New, clean clothes, and now our Papa would come. I was so happy that I could not go to sleep for a long time. I just kept saying "Thank you, dear God, thank you, dear God," over and over again.

How slowly the next two days passed! We kept running inside to ask what time it was, and for once we could not wait for bedtime and the end of day. Our new dresses had been put away to be clean for Papa.

Finally May 20th arrived. We washed very carefully, even our ears, and cleaned our fingernails. My hair was still a mess, but the rest was fine.

As soon as breakfast was over we starting watching the road. We could see far down the road where it curved around the fjord, flanked here and there by houses and a few trees.

We raced up a wooden ramp to the second floor of the barn where the hay was kept during the winter. The top of the ramp was the highest point we could reach, so we ran up there a hundred times looking at the farthest end of the road. But no Papa.

Dinner was in the middle of the day, and even as we ate we kept darting to the window to check if he was coming.

Mama said that it might be evening before he came, or he may not have been able to get transportation, or maybe the phone message got garbled. We must try not to be impatient or disappointed. He would surely come as soon as he could. He wanted to see us as much as we longed for him.

After dinner we continued looking. We saw many things moving on the road. Once it was a man taking the cow to the bull. Then a man on a bicycle. Then a woman with a grocery bag. Far away we saw another person. Slowly, slowly he grew bigger. No, it was a young man with a backpack. Now another person. It was a man. Could this be Papa?

We stood still and stared so hard that we forgot to blink, and our eyes started burning and watering. He had on a long overcoat, and he walked just the way Papa did. Then he waved. It was Papa!

We shouted up to Mama: "Now he is coming!" Then we raced to meet him.

My sister Odny was first. I was next, then my little sister. She fell and hurt her knees. Normally she would have screamed, but she just got up and continued running with bloody knees.

Mama was past 40 years old, so she could not run very fast, although she tried. After her came my chubby sister Torgunn, and last of all Marit, with the baby buggy.

When we got there we almost collided. He put his arms around all of us. We hugged him everywhere, his legs and arms and neck and head. We almost tipped him over.

That made us laugh, all except Mama. She cried. I thought she was acting strange. How could she cry at this time? Then Papa also cried. Grownups were weird. How could they be sad now?

There they stood in the middle of the road, our parents, hugging each other very tightly and wiping tears. I felt embarrassed and I did not know if I should quit smiling.

Papa said, "I finally found you. I have walked all over, from one place to another, asking for you, a mother with 6 children. Twice I went to the wrong place and found another family with many children.

"I almost gave up, but then I met a man who had seen you here and knew our name. I just hoped I would find you in time. The Allies are losing and the Germans are coming south, so we will probably have to leave soon, but at last we are together."

When we came back to the house Mrs. E. was friendly, so very friendly. She had made waffles and we were all invited to eat in the dining room downstairs.

Papa told us about everything that had happened in Narvik, how the whole center of town was burned to the ground.

Mama asked him about our sister Ingebjørg. Well, the hospital was unharmed, so he thought she was OK. He had not been allowed to visit there.

He had been fleeing from mountain cabin to mountain cabin, almost starved to death. He had feared for his life with all the shooting and fighting all around. Slowly he found his way towards the west, and then south, asking for us everywhere. He often despaired of ever finding us.

He held Vesla and me on his lap, stroked our hair, even my short, horrible mess, kissed our cheeks, hugged us over and over, and said he was so glad to see us. He also noticed our new dresses.

He told us that our home had been burned down, completely. But now we were together again, the whole family except Ingebjørg, and he was sure she too would come as soon as she could.

It had been a very long day, but a very happy one. Papa was back.

11
Moving on to Senja

The Norwegian army base at Korsnes was breaking up, and all the refugees were encouraged to leave. Mama had an older sister living on the island of Senja, far to the north. She thought if we could go there we would probably be safe.

Somehow Papa and Mama made arrangements, and again we were packed on board a fishing boat traveling northward.

It was a dangerous trip, and Mama looked nervous. Any coastal sailing was fraught with danger, as mines had been laid everywhere. This was our problem too. The nights were completely light now, and I seem to remember that one man on board had as his only job to look for mines bobbing in the water.

Another danger was that sea battles were fought all the time. German U-boats prowled everywhere as well as British and German destroyers and battleships. Above threatened the planes.

Our boat followed the coastline, weaving between small and big islands and great ocean rocks, trying to avoid the more traveled routes. How long our journey lasted I don't remember. We did sleep.

It seemed like a very long trip, but at last we chugged into a little bay where Tante Hansine and Onkel Edvin lived. (*Tante* and *Onkel* are the Norwegian words for aunt and uncle.) The engines were turned off, and the anchors cast out. Senjehesten was Mama's birthplace, and where she had spent the first 14 years of her life. At that age she had to leave home, find a job, and make her own living. She had not returned after she married when she was 20. She stood on the deck and just looked and looked. She said it all was familiar, yet she felt like a stranger. Now she pointed to various hills and named them. She remembered where the biggest wild blueberries grew, where they kept the cows grazing during the summer. She showed us the white sand beaches where they had waded in the water with their skirts pulled up. And over there was the knoll where the Saint Hans' fire was burned on midsummer night.

Mama was a wonderful story teller. Before the war came, she used to tell us much about her childhood. She told about people and happenings, and described her home place out there on the coast, facing the North Atlantic ocean.

In one way I felt like I had always been there, living her daily life, walking the cow paths to school, being scared on the long, dark winter days and nights, experiencing her small joys and big sorrows. Our coming to Senjehesten was almost like a homecoming for me as well.

There was no pier, so the men lowered a dinghy from the fishing boat, and one man rowed ashore. We watched him bending forward and putting the oars in the water, then leaning back while pulling the oars. Water dripped from the blades as they were lifted barely above the water, then back in again.

I knew that a good rower should not splash, but slice the oars down, deep enough to get a good push, but not so deep that he had to use more energy than necessary. Rowing was a skill to be learned by practicing. Some day maybe I too would learn it.

On shore he dragged the boat up onto the landing where tree trunks had been placed about two feet apart on the ground, like a ladder partially buried, to make the boat glide more smoothly and easily.

A short while later we saw people coming out from the house, and another boat set out for us. It was early morning. As the boat came closer, Mama spoke. "Edvin, is it you?"

"Yes, Dagny," he answered "it is I."

Mama bent over the railing and said very slowly and in a sad voice: "So it had to be a war that brought me back to my childhood home."

She and the baby, with Vesla and me, were the first to be brought ashore. Papa and the others came on the next trip.

Tante Hansine met us down at the landing. She and Mama hugged and cried. Mama repeated to her, "It took a war for us to see each other again. So many times I wanted to come out here, but with a big family—you understand, don't you? It seemed like I always had a little one at the breast."

"Yes, I understand," said Tante Hansine.

She looked like Mama, only much older. Her hair was gray and slicked back into a bun. She wore a dark, flower-printed dress, and a white apron in front. The skin on her hands was red and shiny and wrinkled. She was almost 60 years old. Mama used to say that Hansine was the prettiest of them all. There were five sisters and two brothers still living, but my mother's mother had given birth to twelve children.

To me Shirley Temple and Deanna Durbin were pretty. They were film stars in a place very far away called Hollywood. It was in America, way over on the other side of the Atlantic Ocean. One of Mama's brothers had been there, in a place called Canada.

Tante Hansine did not look pretty to me, but she looked very, very kind, just like a grandmother. I had always wanted to have a grandmother, but both mine had died long before I was born.

She hugged us gently, smiled, and asked what our names were, although she already knew them. Then she told us to come in and meet our cousins, and get something to eat.

Finally we had come to people who were family, who did not call us refugees and let us know that we were just trouble, but who seemed glad to see us. I felt so lighthearted inside.

12

Norway's Last Front

The German occupation forces continued their push from the coastal cities into the fjords and valleys of Norway. A poorly prepared and ill-equipped Norwegian army resisted bravely and bitterly, in some areas assisted by British and French/Polish troops. But a combination of rugged terrain, grim weather, harsh conditions and lack of coordination led to one Allied defeat after another.

The Germans established bases and built airports. *Die Luftwaffe* pummeled the Allies from the air, and parachuted supplies and fresh troops in an unending stream.

King Håkon, the legitimate government and all the gold reserves from the Bank of Norway continued the flight north. So did companies of the Norwegian army which were still undefeated.

By the beginning of May most of the southern part of Norway was a conquered and occupied territory while Northern Norway was still actively at war.

Along this long stretched land, fierce battles were fought in the hills and mountains. Against the Germans stood a collection of Norwegian military groups from many parts of the country. With them were the British 24th Guard Brigade, three battalions of French *Chausseurs Alpins,* two battalions of the French Foreign legion, who were mostly Spaniards, and four battalions of Polish troops.

At sea German U-boats prowled and blew up warships and merchant vessels while they themselves in turn were torpedoed and destroyed by the Allies.

After the defeats in the South, the Allies' thrust was to recapture and retain control of Narvik and the iron ore. All the forces gathered in this area, and the bloodiest battles of the war were carried on here.

While the Allied land forces pushed towards Narvik from the northwest, east and south in an ever-tightening noose, the city and surroundings were being bombarded from air and sea, day in and day out. German planes went for the seagoing vessels and the Allied land forces. The Allies pelted the German installations from battleships and from the air.

Most civilians in Narvik had fled, but a few thousand still remained. At the hospital, the staff worked as doggedly as ever. The electricity had been cut off. Water and food were scarce. My sister said they were so hungry and tired that a sense of hopelessness and even despair fell on them.

On April 20th Ingebjørg ventured out to see if she could contact Papa on the ferry, which was still operating. As she walked down the hill towards the ferry dock, she was stopped by a German guard. He waved her away with his rifle. She turned around and walked back slowly, feeling totally dejected.

Every so often she would turn around and look at the ferry that was just moving out from the dock. She followed it with her eyes. Suddenly a British warship came in sight, and before she knew it the ferry went down. Stunned she stood there, 19 years old, alone, numb with shock and grief. *"Adjø, Far,"* she whispered. Goodbye, Father.

Part of her duties at the hospital was to go out and look for wounded who needed help. One day while she was doing this, suddenly the explosions started again, so she crawled in by the school wall and huddled there. A bunch of German horses, frantic with fear, came galloping towards her. At the last moment they veered past her with such force and speed that large chunks of muddy dirt rained over her. She was sure she was going to be killed by flying hooves.

Another duty was to stand guard on the hospital roof, watching for airplanes. Her vision was good so she could tell their nationality from the wing markings, even from a long distance. She would rush downstairs to give the alarm, so they could take appropriate action.

With all the bombing and shooting, fires erupted everywhere. Most of the town's buildings were made of wood. High up in the church tower men kept a 24-hour watch so they could alert the tiny fire department and volunteers who would rush out. Most of the time their efforts were in vain. Large parts of the city burned.

On May 28th, after horrendous battles on every hill and mountainside around Narvik, the city was freed. General Dietl and his men had been pushed up along Ofotbanen towards the Swedish border. Soon they would be captured. Jubilation erupted in the streets as Norwegians, British, French and Polish mingled in joyous celebration. The Germans had destroyed everything they could before retreating. This included the whole iron transport and shipping system, tracks, railroad cars and locomotives, crushers and piers.

Destruction of the transport system: (above) Locomotive. Iron ore railroad cars. (below) Railroad bridge. Iron ore loading dock.

But sane heads knew that the retaliation would be swift. It came on June 2nd. On a beautiful, sunny day huge German planes came sailing in over the city and let go of their deadly load. Systematically they fire-bombed the already crippled city. It seemed that the whole world was burning, and the blue sky changed into a black, ominous gloom.

The civilian population still in Narvik was urged to leave. Most went westward to islands and small communities. A few were able to get to Sweden through Red Cross arrangements. Some got on British ships. Only a skeleton crew remained at the hospital to take care of the wounded. My sister was able to get on a little fishing boat with her bicycle and a small bundle of personal belongings. Now she began her search for us, her family.

Hitler had attacked The Netherlands, Belgium and Luxembourg on May 10th. After Belgium surrendered May 28th, British, French and Belgian troops retreated to Dunkerque on the northern French coast. Here the famous rescue took place, where more than 336 thousand men waded out to British ships of all kinds, including fishing boats and motor boats, and were brought safely to England. France was attacked by Germany June 5th, and the French force was in retreat.

The Allies felt that they could no longer keep forces tied up in Northern Norway. Narvik had become low on British priorities. And so the orders came to evacuate. This was bitter news. During June 6th and 7th, 25thousand Allied forces were pulled out. The King, Prime Minister Nygaardsvold's government, Norway's gold reserves and a great many Norwegians left for England. They promised to continue the war from outside the country's border. But for those left behind it was a heartbreaking and intensely harsh disappointment.

And so Norway was taken. On June 9th General Dietl and his men again took possession of Narvik.

Officially the cost to Germany of the two month fighting in Norway was 1,317 killed and 2,375 lost at sea. The British lost 4,400, the Norwegians 1,335, the French and Poles 530. Today military cemeteries in Narvik and Ankenes with their rows and rows of white crosses and stone monuments are silent memorials to Norway's last front.

13
On the Island of Senja

Tante Hansine had ten children. Only the youngest, Ellinor, was unmarried. The rest of them were living in their own houses, some close by, others farther away. Her oldest son Ewald was just six years younger than Mama. He had two girls a bit older than I was. They had to help their mother all the time, carrying water, cooking dinner, washing dishes, washing floors, cleaning the ashes out of the stove, bringing in dried slices of peat which was what they burned instead of wood and coal. They even knew how to feed and milk the cow. I admired them very much, for, with four older sisters, I was not used to doing much work.

Before the war my older sisters did everything Mama could not find time to do. Once in a while I might go to the store to buy some little thing, like yeast for baking, a piece of cheese, syrup or margarine, but we did not buy very much. We had fish and potatoes, carrots and rutabagas in the cellar. Mama baked all our bread.

Every morning I walked to my godmother's house for milk. She had cows. We paid for the milk every time Papa's wages came in. We also had wild blueberry and lingonberry jam in big containers. Mama and my big sisters picked berries in August and September—many, many liters of each kind—up in the hills and mountainside.

Up to now my life had been one of play and school. School was from 8:30 in the morning till 1:00 in the afternoon. We had some homework in the evenings, but the whole afternoon was spent outside playing.

We made up games, using whatever we could find outdoors as toys. For hopscotch we used flat, smooth rocks, and sticks to make the pattern in the hard soil.

We played farm. Our animals were various kinds of sea shells. We called them horse shells and cow shells, sheep and goat shells, rooster and chicken shells. Twigs were used to build pens to keep them in, and we pretended to feed and water our livestock, and clean out the messes they made.

We built roads and rivers, dams and docks, with cars, trucks and boats in constant motion. Pieces of wood could become many things.

In certain places we could dig for clay. This we kneaded and molded into breads and cakes. It also worked well for cups and plates, pots and pans, anything we needed for playing at housekeeping. The clay hardened quickly.

We kept a store where we sold and weighed sand and dirt, various grasses and leaves, pebbles and rocks, pretending all to be food. For money we used a special kind of grass.

If we knew someone with a long rope or a real rubber ball, we would walk long distances in order to play jump rope and ball games And of course we played tag, hide and seek, and many song games. The winter brought many other kinds of activities. I cannot remember ever being bored.

Even as refugees we tried to maintain our normal days. Whenever we came to a new place, we found new playmates and from them we might learn new games, or different variations of the old ones.

One sunny day Mama was sitting with us on a grassy knoll. She seemed to have more time now. Suddenly she picked up five round rocks, each about the size of a small cherry tomato. She taught us to play a game called "Five-stone." It was sort of a juggling game, like jacks, throwing one or more rocks in the air while quickly picking up the ones that were left on the ground, and catching the airborne ones before they fell. This was a game she had played as a girl. I thought it was so special. I practiced and practiced, and took good care of the five smooth rocks that were mine.

In Senjehesten we stayed at Ewald's house. One day while we were there Mama was looking out the window towards my Aunt's place when she saw Papa standing in the middle of the road hugging and patting the back of a strange woman. Who in the world was that? They just stood there for the longest time hanging on to each other. Such unusual behavior!

Finally they started walking closer, Papa holding on to a bike. Ingebjørg! It was Ingebjørg. Our oldest sister had found us at last!

She had bicycled from Narvik to Harstad because we had an aunt and uncle there, and she thought they might know what had happened to us. It was a long journey. She was weak, hungry and tired when she started out and her food supply was scarce. She knew the road went over mountains and through valleys, across fjords and wooded areas.

One day she passed a little white house with a most wonderful odor of freshly fried fish cakes streaming through the open windows. She stopped and knocked on the door. A crabby lady appeared. Ingebjørg asked if she could buy a couple of fish cakes. "Where do you come from?" the lady asked sternly.

Ingebjørg told her she had bicycled from Narvik where she had been working at the hospital during the whole two months of war, and now she was trying to find her family.

When the woman heard that, her stern expression changed. She put the whole platter of fish cakes on the table, and urged my sister to eat all she wanted. It was the first real meal she had eaten in a very long time. She ate until she could hold no more. Then she went outside and vomited. Still, she thought of this as her first good experience since the war started.

When she finally reached Harstad, our aunt and uncle were not there. She walked the bike down to the pier, where she met a teacher from Narvik. She wondered if he knew where we were. Yes, he knew, and a fishing boat down the pier was just ready to take off for Skrolsvik on Senja. She hurried on board with her bike and bundle. She was finally going to be with her family again.

From Skrolsvik down to Senjehesten was not a long way, but the road was terrible, really just a cow path. It was rutty and narrow, full of rocks and holes and bumps. Ingebjørg got on the bike and pedaled as fast as she could, with her tongue hanging out. She rattled and shook and flew, veering to the left and right, down, down the hills.

Then she saw Tante Hansine's house. Some people were outside, and my God, out in the road, a little closer, was Papa! But it could not be. He was dead. With her own eyes she had seen the ferry go down. But Papa was alive!

She jumped off the bike, put it down on the ground and threw her arms around him. Then she started crying, sobbing loudly, without being able to stop. Papa just held her and patted her back gently. For a long time they stood there, until she had calmed down. The crying started again when Mama came out.

Bjørg, as we called her, had always been slender, but now she was really skinny. She just cried and cried, and Mama said she needed a lot of quiet and rest. She had to stay in bed for several days, and we tiptoed around. When she got up again she did not want to talk about what had happened in the hospital except to say it was terrible.

Tante Hansine had a leg wound that would not heal. Bjørg was asked to take a look at it. After all she was a nurse's aide, and so she must know a lot. She cleaned up the wound, changed the dressings every day, and Tante's leg healed up. Afterwards she always said that Bjørg had saved her leg.

On the island of Senja the beaches were beautiful. Instead of gray and black pebbles they were made of white, grainy sand. It was so much fun walking barefoot there—the sand just tickled our feet. It did not hurt and cut like the stones on the beaches at home. The shells were also different. They were pink, or had a rainbow shine. We could almost look through them. There were cone-shaped ones, and spiral ones where we could hear the sound of the ocean when we held them to our ear. I really liked hunting along those beaches. Wild caraway plants grew along the edges, and we filled our pockets with their seeds, relishing the strong, spicy taste.

But there was sadness too. As the war and the sea battles continued, heavy, black oil came floating in. Often we saw dead birds, or birds that were covered with black, sticky stuff. They would try to fly, or run along, but perhaps only one wing would work, or there were thick globs hanging on their feet, and so they stumbled and fell, and finally became still. We felt very sad and helpless watching them.

On June 7th we learned that Norway had capitulated to the Germans. We were now an occupied country. All these words were new and strange. We learned that our royal family had fled to England with the government, and now we had a new government, which was not really a government.

But Quisling was out of it. People were glad at that, but shook their heads and wondered what was in store for us from now on.

I remember feeling very sad deep inside that we had lost the war. Our country was no longer ours, but belonged to the Germans.

I still had not met any of them. I wondered what they looked like.

14

Quisling and the Germans

After the fighting in Northern Norway ended, we learned more details of the collapse of our country during these two terrible months.

On April 9th confusion reigned. The Germans had occupied several key ports, and were spreading quickly into the country. The King and his family, together with Prime Minister Nygaardsvold and his government, were in flight northward. So were all of Norway's gold reserves—1542 containers totaling almost 60,000 kilos. The story of this transport from Oslo to Tromsø is almost unbelievable, and books have been written about that alone.

On the evening of April 9th, from *Norsk Rikskringkasting* (NRK), the state-operated broadcasting center in Oslo which had been taken over by the Germans, Quisling declared that he had formed a national government with himself as the leader.

But the local radio stations in non-occupied areas told of resistance towards the Germans and hinted that the British Navy would attack and that the British invasion was at hand.

Panic gripped the population. Stores and offices closed and people feared a civil war. Men, women and children fled the cities and heavily populated areas in great haste, not really knowing where to go, but seeking safety in the countryside and smaller towns.

Already, the day after the invasion, the chief justice of the Supreme Court, Pål Berg, called on the other justices in Oslo.

They thought it would be better to negotiate with the Germans to work out a compromise where Norwegians would have some input and control rather than leave all administration to the Germans. They knew the Germans had little confidence in Quisling's ability to govern the country.

On April 15th Pål Berg read a proclamation over NRK. He said that under these extraordinary circumstances the Supreme Court had found it necessary to form an *Administrasjons Råd* (Administrative Council) to lead the civil administration of the occupied portions of Norway. He trusted that the King would approve of these measures. He announced that Quisling would step down as leader of the government, but would lead the demobilization of the Norwegian military in occupied areas. Quisling's first reign had lasted six days.

This Administrative Council of seven well-known and highly regarded Norwegians, together with ten governmental departments took over the civil government of Norway from April 15th. Most people nodded their heads and felt relieved that good Norwegians were still in charge, and Quisling was not.

But then on April 24th Josef Terboven arrived in Oslo from Germany. Hitler had told him to, "Act in such a way that you win the Norwegian people to me." He was to have the ultimate authority of the civil administration of Norway. His title was *"Reichskommisar fur die bestzten Gebiete Norwegens"* (State Commisioner for Occupied Norway).

His tasks were, first, to advance Germany's total war. This meant that Norway would supply whatever it was capable of for the war machine—workers, material, food. Second, he was to organize the Norwegian government so it would respond to German pressure to keep the population under control.

A third, unofficial, task was to keep an eye on General von Falkenhorst, the Commander of all the German forces in Norway. Von Falkenhorst was not a member of the Nazi party in Germany, and because of this was thought to need some supervision. Josef Terboven wielded absolute power in Norway.

As the spring and summer of 1940 progressed and more and more of Norway was occupied by Germans, the Administrative Council's work became increasingly difficult. They had to cover a larger territory and be responsible for more people. Also, Terboven and his specialists involved themselves to an ever greater degree in governing Norway.

They forced the Administrative Council to divide Norway into sections with territorial borders which could not be crossed without travel permits. They held press conferences telling the newspapers what they could print:

• All reports of German losses and Allied victories were forbidden.
• No coverage of speeches by the King or the Nygaardsvold government was allowed, nor any pictures of the King.
• There was to be no criticism of German authorities.
• All NRK broadcasting was censored, and a Nazi journalist was in charge of the foreign news department, NTB.
• All foreign news was to be commented on "in the German spirit."
• Only good economic news and improved conditions could be reported.

Terboven also went outside the Administrative Council to establish rules and regulations directly to local officials in various areas.

On May 27 he proclaimed that all political meetings were forbidden, except those of NS (*Nasjonal Samling,* the National Unity, or the Norwegian Nazi political party). Five days later he challenged the Norwegians to take the initiative in finding new ways to cooperate with the Germans.

As soon as the King and Nygaardsvold government left for England on June 7, Terboven called in the Administrative Council and the leaders of the four major political parties. The King had sent a proclamation to the Norwegian people as he was leaving, saying that neither he nor his government would give up the fight for Norway's independence and freedom. On the contrary they would fight on outside Norway's borders. This was in reality a declaration of war against the Germans.

Terboven forced the leaders of the parties to establish a special government State Council, ousting the Nygaardsvold government. They were also to ask the King to abdicate.

The King responded that the request was unconstitutional and had been drafted under pressure from a foreign power.

He said that he had been chosen to be Norway's King by the Norwegian people, and would only abdicate if it became clear that this was the wish of the people.

He could not accept any government that was established contrary to Norway's Constitution and forced upon his people. "The Norwegian people's freedom and independence is the first command of Norway's Law, and I will follow this commandment and look after the interests of the Norwegian people by maintaining the position and the duty given to me by a free people in 1905."

The King's answer spread like wildfire throughout the country. It was first heard from BBC London, was written down and duplicated by the thousands.

It was the first big illegal publication of the war. It passed from neighbor to neighbor, from friend to friend, so soon every person in Norway knew why the King could not abdicate.

This proved to be a rallying point for the Norwegian people. They were angered that the King had been asked to abdicate, and were determined to maintain their loyalty to him and the legally elected government, although they were exiled. Håkon the Seventh became the symbol of freedom and independence.

We were sure that somehow he would be able to "continue the fight" and in the end restore Norway to its normal state. He was still our King, and we his people.

15

Harstad: We Meet Germans

We spent the summer of 1940 on the island of Senja. The school house had rooms upstairs for any children who lived too far away from home to go back and forth every day. They lived at the school the whole school year. Now that the school was no longer in session, we were allowed to live there. Living in a school building was strange, but at least we were not imposing on anyone.

The kitchen was very large, everything much bigger than normal. The kettles and pots and pans were giant, and the soup ladles and spatulas and other utensils were also huge. The dishes we ate from were white and heavy. Papa, who had gone back to work, sent money regularly now, so we could buy our own food, whatever was available. Mama's family helped with fish and meat and potatoes.

Since we were the only refugees in that community, we were watched closely—not in an unfriendly way but out of curiosity. People asked us children many questions. When the whole family went out walking, we saw people behind the curtains peering at us. It was really interesting and fun to be almost famous.

The war continued in Europe and other places in the world, but the fighting had stopped in Norway after the capitulation. Towards the end of the summer our parents decided that we should move to a place where we could go to school, since we could not stay in our present place anyway. Our next move was to Harstad. Unlike Narvik, this city had not been destroyed.

We rented the first floor of a newer home, a light and pleasant apartment with a modern kitchen, and two other rooms. We had no furniture, but little by little we bought beds and chairs and a table, most of them used. At last we had a real home again.

In Harstad I saw "the Germans" for the first time. I was quite surprised. They looked just the same as we did, not like monsters. They spoke a language we could not understand. They wore gray-green uniforms. I noticed that they had different kinds of uniforms. All had pants and jackets with a leather belt. The collars were black with a white rectangle in the corners. They had four pockets with metal buttons, and one row of metal buttons in front. Above the right top pocket was a metal eagle.

Some of the soldiers wore heavy shoes, others had long, black boots. The hats were different too. Some looked like the kind we used to make out of folded newspaper. Others had brims. Some of the hats came up high in front. They belonged to the officers who also often wore riding pants, ballooning out above their long boots.

The guards who walked in front of buildings usually had on long, belted coats, and they wore helmets. On one shoulder they carried a strange kind of gun. It was not like the hunting rifle I had seen in the glass-door cupboard in one of my friend's home, but looked like a "T" with the stem sticking out and the top of the "T" and fastened with a leather strap around the shoulder. At times they carried hand grenades from the belt. On top of the shoulders were epaulets with colorful markings. The officers usually had rows of colored decorations on their chest.

They walked with firm, determined steps, kind of stiffly, and when they met each other they lifted one arm straight out and a little bit up and said, *"Heil."*

The elementary school stood right below our apartment, facing the main road. It was taken over by what people called *Okkupasjons Makten* (the occupation forces). That is, the Germans who lived there. High up on the flag pole flew, not the Norwegian flag, but a red flag with a white circle in the middle, and on the white circle a black design called a swastika. It did not seem right to me. A Norwegian flag pole with a German flag!

The soldiers were everywhere—on the streets and in the stores, on the docks and in the buses. If they spoke to us or smiled at us, we were supposed to turn our faces away, for they were the enemy. When we did so they laughed at us, made fun of us, we thought.

They had big trucks with darkish green canvas covers in back. The trucks smelled funny. Often these were full of soldiers, sitting on benches with their guns sticking straight up between their knees. I also saw the biggest horses I had ever seen, pulling large wagons. My, did those horses have huge feet!

The Germans liked to sing. They marched a lot and sang a lot. All their arms and legs were moving at the same time in the same direction. If I stared at them, it looked like a machine with movable parts. Sometimes they would kick their legs up stiffly in front of them. After a while we learned many of their songs. The words were a little bit like Norwegian, only twisted, and often we could guess what they meant:

"Wenn wir fahren, wenn wir fahren, wenn wir fahren gegen Engeland, Engeland," or "When we go, when we go, when we go towards England, England."

It was not so hard.

Then there were signs in German posted on buildings or telephone poles: *Haltung! Eintritt verboten!* That meant: Halt! Entrance forbidden!

We learned lots of words and expressions. I don't know how we did it, but we picked them up somehow, and bandied them around: *"Du bisst verruckt. Du bisst ein Dumkopf. Ich bin krank."* etc. (You're crazy! You're a dumbhead! I'm sick.)

There was a swear word which sounded really strong and exciting: *"Donnerwetter!"* (thunderweather). If we said that with great explosive force it could truly express how angry we felt. And somehow we did not feel that we said something wrong, because the word did not mean anything bad in Norwegian.

Terboven was in charge of everything. He lived in Oslo, the capital of Norway. I heard people talking about *Nyordninga* (The New Order). I did not really understand what it meant, but I knew that it was different from before the war started. Another new word was *Nasifisering* (Nazification). People did not like it, and often said: "God alone knows what is going to happen to us." Every time I heard it my stomach got that funny, achy feeling. I was afraid, but I did not know what I had done wrong.

The Germans were in charge, and all the time there were new rules. It became illegal to gather in front of any place where the Germans lived. We could no longer get up from a bus seat when a Nazi or German sat down next to us, or pretend that something was stuck in our throat when we passed a *Hird* (one of Quisling's storm troopers) or a German. All demonstrations were illegal.

Mother told us to be careful and not do anything that could get us or our family in trouble. My sister Torgunn stayed with Onkel Jens and Tante Magda in Harstad. She helped them out in the house, and earned a little money as well.

One Sunday night they came out to visit us. As they passed the school below, the guard stepped out and shouted, *"Haltung!"* It seemed they always shouted or talked loudly. The guard shone a flashlight in their faces and demanded to know where they were going. My sister pointed up the hill and said, *"Meine Mutter"* (my mother). They were allowed to pass. I remember that my sister was very upset.

One night someone knocked hard on our front door. Mama opened. A German shouted, *"Das Papier!"* *"Dass"* is a slang word for toilet or outhouse, so *"dasspapir"* is toilet paper in Norwegian. This seemed funny to us. Mother did not understand. He stepped into the kitchen with his heavy boots, walked to the window where the new, black blinds were pulled down. Again he said something about *Das Papier*. Then we understood. There was a gap on the side of the paper blackout blinds, and a little light had escaped. That was not acceptable.

After he left Mama said, *"O, gå nu bare, du og ditt dasspapir."* "Oh, just go now, you and your toilet paper."

For five years we had these soldiers around us. We called them only *"Tyskertan"* ("the Germans" in dialect). I cannot recall a single German face. They were bodies in a uniform to me, but I looked at them furtively, with a mixture of fear and dislike, curiosity and fascination.

I knew that their presence made life more difficult for us.

Vesla (Kirsten) and Hanna,
Harstad, Winter 1941

16
The New Order

On September 25th, 1940, Terboven spoke to the Norwegian people. First he declared friendship on behalf of the German people to the Norwegians. Then he complained about the lack of cooperation from our side. Finally he stated the consequences of this failing:

• The Royal House will not return to Norway.
• The Nygaardsvold government likewise.
• Any activity in favor of the exiled King and government is prohibited. The traditional church prayer for the King and his house said during the liturgy is to be discontinued.
• The activity of the Administrative Council is terminated.
• Thirteen state commissioners are appointed to take over the government business as of today. Each will be the leader of one department, and directly responsible only to Terboven.
• All political parties are abolished, except NS, the Nazi party. There is only one way, and it goes through NS.

Quisling, as leader of the party, was given a group of German advisors, called *Einsatzstab* (implementation staff). They were to guide Quisling politically, help him build up NS more speedily, and lay out the propaganda. Terboven regarded Quisling "only as an insignificant outsider" who unfortunately had some support from Hitler himself, and therefore could not just be removed. But he kept close tab on him, using his *Sicherheitsdients* (security service) to gather and file all reports on Quisling's undertakings. If Quisling could not deliver, he might be expendable.

The Germans wanted peaceful conditions in Norway. They did not want to use their military forces for peacekeeping. They wanted our fish and cod liver oil, our paper and iron ore, our ports and bases for access to the Atlantic. They especially needed our workers. And Terboven planned to use NS as his vehicle to get what he wanted.

The propaganda became heavy. All over the country Quisling and his men traveled to proclaim *Nyordninga* (the New Order). It included a fundamental change in the district and local governments as well. Free elections would be replaced by the *Nazi Fører Prinsipp* (Nazi Leader Principle) with power to come from above, not from the people. For example, the Department of the Interior would assume the authority to evaluate, suspend and dismiss all government officials. Qualification for office was membership in NS.

One problem was that few men had that qualification. NS was a small party, poorly organized with about 4,000 members at the end of 1939. Most of the functioning officials in county and district did not belong to NS. They sent letters expressing their concern about "the destruction of communal self-government which in the people's mind is fundamental to Norwegian administration." These letters were ignored.

Gradually the old officials were replaced by NS people. Many joined the party in name only to keep their places, and not a few so they could secretly work against the Nazi system. The highest official NS membership was around 42,000 in 1943. It declined from then on, but it still was less than one and a half per cent of Norway's population.

The Nazi-Quisling control increased. The King and *Storting* (parliament) had been abolished. Only the Supreme Court was still intact. It protested Terboven's claim to supplant Norwegian Law. That was against the Hague Convention and international law. One of the judges was arrested "for political activities against the state." Terboven next tried to force the rest of the judges to retire, by lowering the age of eligibility. When this failed he issued a proclamation: "Neither the Supreme Court nor any other Norwegian judiciary can take a position on a question of the validity of the ordinances issued by the Reichscommissar or the authority established on September 28th, 1940." In protest all the judges of the Supreme Court resigned on December 12, 1940. Nazi judges of questionable qualifications were appointed.

This was another wake-up call for the country. The general adult population was always more or less politically aware. Now a feeling of shock and shame and bewilderment pervaded every part of the land. But there was no way to express the anger and feelings of frustration. No political parties.

In Norway individuals do not run for election. The party does, and the party officials appoint persons who have proved themselves worthy to represent the voters in the government, all segments of it. My parents voted for the party and its policy. I overheard them talking many times, but was too young to understand. My father usually voted *Arbeiderpartiet* (Labor), my mother was leaning more towards *Høyre* (Right).

Now there was only the NS, and no elections. The radio and newspapers were censored and under German control. The Norwegian police was trying to be loyal to their own people, but they were under great pressure. In mid-December they were ordered to use the Hitler-greeting, the open hand, raised arm *Heil!*

There were protests, at first in small ways. Mysteriously, graffiti blossomed: "Down with Quisling," "Long live H7!" This symbol, an "H" with a "7" over the cross-bar, for King Håkon VII, could be seen in many places. It was painted into decorative designs, knitted into scarves, mittens, sweaters and caps. In the corner of paper money was scribbled "To hell with NS!" The red hat of the *Nisse,* the Norwegian pixie or elf became a symbol of protest. A *jøssing* was a loyal Norwegian, and soon there was a *jøssing* uniform: a special kind of sweater and the *nisse* hat.

Paper clips in the coat lapel meant "we are holding together." A comb visible in a pocket meant "we can take care of ourselves." Labels such as "Made in Norway," "100% Norwegian," "Norwegian Product." etc. were prominently displayed. The red, white and blue crossed flag or colors were worn on coat collars.

The *Hird* ripped these signs of protest off collars and lapels, and might find a protestor's razor blade attached to the back side. Too bad!

Many skirmishes took place in the dark streets at night between young Norwegian men and the *Hird*. When Nazi leaders traveled around the country to give speeches, a great number of people would gather outside the meeting places. Inside the halls were empty. Outside they would sing the national hymn and national anthem, shout the King's motto "All for Norway" and *"Vi vil vinne"* (we will win). They greeted each other with two fingers raised forming the V-for-Victory sign. They also blew whistles and made a loud racket.

When some were arrested, the anger of the population grew. Soon small acts of sabotage started taking place. Just as the speaker was about to start his propaganda spiel, a loudspeaker would explode or the electricity fail. Car tires were slashed. A German soldier had acid thrown in his face. On buses, street cars and trains, people would get up from their seats and stand if a *Hird* or NS member or German sat next to them. Coughing, as if something was stuck in the throat, or pinching one's nose to keep out a bad smell was also practiced when passing the enemy on the street.

The newspapers became adept at writing "between the lines." They would have curious typographical errors which changed the meaning of the propaganda. Once the headline was "Utterly Fantastic!" Underneath was a paragraph quoting one of the Nazis telling that the growth of the Nazi party lately was utterly fantastic. Another time the headline said: "We Would Like to Wring Their Necks." Underneath was a large picture of Terboven and his men. Next to the picture a narrow column of print reported the theft of some rationing cards. The editors could claim they were outraged by the theft.

Children also understood. There were funny cartoons with hidden meanings. I remember a strange looking picture of a pig. If we cut it out and folded it in a certain way, it became a picture of Hitler. A little boy wrote in an essay on cats: "When Håkon the Seventh was King in Norway, all the cats were happy."

Another visited the museum near Oslo where Nansen's ship Fram was displayed. A German guard said, "That is a small ship." The boy answered, "Yes. But it got them to England every time." He had learned of the use of fishing boats for the Underground activities between England and Norway.

Humor was one way of coping. The New Order became a joke, so that anytime anything did not go as planned people would wink and laugh at each other and say, "It must be *Nyordninga,*" the New Order.

But it was not much of a laughing matter. Quisling declared in a speech November 8th, "We will force our vision through with all means that become necessary. It may be necessary to replace the silk gloves with something that can be better understood."

On November 27th, the German propaganda minister Goebbels arrived in Norway. Officially he came to see how the German troops were doing, but Berlin was aware of the friction in Norway, and sent the propaganda chief to check things out. As he traveled up the main street in the capital a group of university students were lined up on the side. When he passed in front of them, they abruptly turned their backs to him. They were arrested immediately.

The newspapers appealed for an end to demonstrations. The Nazi paper *Fritt Folk* threatened that if these demonstrations did not stop "we will hit back, hit so hard that they will lose both sight and hearing."

General von Falkenhorst sent secret instructions to his *Wehrmacht,* "The Norwegian attitude has worsened lately. Stay out of political battles and discussions. Move carefully, and stay away from demonstrations and altercations. Only Gestapo and Norwegian police shall intercede, because they have been instructed in how to proceed. If there is danger for the troops or their supply, or demonstrations against Germany and *Der Führer* they will attack, severely and powerfully. Firing in the crowd may be necessary."

The season of darkness was ahead, both in the Northern Norway winters and throughout our occupied country.

17
Third Grade in Harstad. 1940-1941

Since the Germans had occupied all the school buildings, we had to go to school in private homes. If someone had a large bedroom or an extra room it was requisitioned for education.

I started third grade with a completely new and unknown group of children, but soon made friends with some of them. The father of one of the girls was a baker. Her mother was dead, so Beate would go to the bakery after school. I really liked being invited to go with her, because we would get to eat the "cake peelings." After the cakes and pastries were baked her father would cut off all the uneven or over-baked parts, and they tasted delicious.

At this time of the occupation, supplies of white flour, sugar, and butter were still available to the civilian population, although they were rationed. Each person in the family had many cards with little squares which would be cut off every time we bought milk, flour, sugar, margarine, soap, clothing or whatever. With many members in our family, we often had more cards than money to buy with, so Mama would give away a lot. Some people would trade their cards for things they wanted. This *klire* or bartering was considered a little bit wrong.

What I remember from third grade is the house we had school in. It sat up on a hill, close to a tuberculosis sanatorium. We could see the patients being wheeled out on big stretchers to lie in the fresh air. Many children had this disease, and every year we would be tested for it. A nurse would come to the class room, scratch three marks with a tiny knife on the skin of our forearm. Then she smeared something brown and strong smelling on the scratches. In a few days she came back to see if they had swelled up. That was called being positive. If they did we would have to go in for a chest X-ray. If not, we were negative, and glad.

The lady who owned the house often came out during recess to talk with us. She asked us what we wanted to become when we grew up. I wanted to be either a teacher or a mission doctor. I liked reading stories about doctors from Norway who went to Africa and India to help the people.

In Harstad I had a friend named Lise. She was retarded. I felt sorry for her because some of the children made fun of her. She had yellow hair, a short neck and a long face. Lise and I liked to go to the Salvation Army meetings. We loved their uniforms, and their happy music. They played guitar, mandolin, accordion and trumpet, and their songs were fast and joyous and made me feel like tapping my feet. I could not do that, for that would be wrong. They talked about Jesus who loves the sinners, and asked people to come forward to receive him. Some of the people who went forward cried and looked very sad. Lise and I also went up to the kneeling bench, but the Salvation Army people said we did not need to because we were children, and the Kingdom of Heaven belonged to us anyway. So after that we just went there to listen to the happy music.

That winter we built a large snow house in our yard. In the early dark afternoons we sat inside with a candle flickering, a whole bunch of children. The boys, and sometimes the girls, told dirty stories. I was all eyes and ears, for now I learned about the secret world the adults in my life inhabited. But somehow I rejected the idea that my parents "did it." I said that when I was grown up I would never be part of that. "Oh yes, you have to, if you are going to become a mama," they told me. Well, I thought, that is a long time ahead in the future, and maybe by then I could figure out a different way.

But there was so much new to think about. First the war and the Germans, then Jesus and sin, dirty words and sex, and this whole thing called the future, and of course school.

I liked school, where learning was easy for me. My friend Lise hated school. She was a year older than I and still she was only in second grade. I could read books, and she had difficulty reading signs and simple sentences. It seemed so strange to me. Lise lived with her grandparents. So did her mother and aunt who were twins. Lise's mother was unmarried. She did not know who or where her dad was. I heard Mama talking to my sisters about them, that they were all retarded, and somehow that was not a good thing to be. But they didn't seem different to me and I liked them because they were always very friendly to me.

Lise's grandmother told stories about the subterranean people in Norwegian folklore who are called *Huldrefolket*. Mama also told stories about them. We spent many evenings listening to these tales that had passed from generation to generation.

18
Huldrefolket (The Hulder People)

"A long time ago, when Adam and Eve were the first parents, God used to visit them on a regular basis. Eve had many children, and once when God came to visit she felt embarrassed to show him all her children, so she hid some of them. God told her that what she had hidden would forever remain hidden, and that was the beginning of the Hulder people."

This is what an old lady told me when I was visiting her out in the country. She was a healer. She could heal people by putting her hands on them, and could stop massive bleeding from severe cuts. Sick people would travel long distances to be healed by her.

She believed that the Hulder people lived in hillocks and underground, and that once in a while they would show themselves to humans. They were very beautiful and looked just like us except they had a cow tail, and that was how you could tell who they were.

Lise's grandmother also believed in their existence. She said she had seen them herself. This is one story she told us:

"I was a young girl guarding the cows and goats while they grazed up in the hills. One day I suddenly felt dizzy, so I sat down in the heather. Then I saw him, a very good-looking young man between the birch trees. He had blue eyes and fair hair. He wore black trousers with silver buckles beneath the knees. His shirt was shiny white, and his blue vest had silver buttons. His face was lit up in a beautiful smile.

"I thought that perhaps he was a Hulder boy, but I could not see the cow tail behind him. He asked if I would like something to eat, and I answered the truth for I was always hungry. He took me by my hand and pulled me up from the heather. Then we walked together in between the trees, and there was the door to his *"gamme."* This is a dwelling set into a hillside, and made of sod.

"He opened the door, and we stepped inside. It was a rich man's house, I could tell. The table had been set with the finest dishes and silverware, and oh, such wonderful food! On the walls hung many lovely tapestries, and more silver platters and bowls. In the corner stood a silver spinning wheel. By now I realized that this was indeed a Hulder home.

"I knew that if I tasted any of the food, I would be caught forever and ever underground. I would never be able to see my parents again, or enter into the world of the Christian people. The boy lifted a plate full of the finest bread and cheese to me, and oh, how tempting it was, for I was very hungry.

" But I closed my eyes, folded my hands and started praying, 'Our Father who art in Heaven.' Then I heard a big bang, and felt a great wind blowing over me. When I opened my eyes I was sitting in the heather again. The boy and all his things had vanished, but I heard the sound of someone crying, and I just caught sight of a cow tail disappearing behind the trees.

"This was the first time they tried to bewitch me. Many times later I saw them with their beautiful herds of fat, red cows—the girls in their long, blue dresses, singing such soft songs, while their golden hair flowed over their shoulders. But always I was able to see the cow tails hanging down beneath their dresses, so I quickly said the Lord's Prayer, and they would be gone again, unable to cast their spell over me.

"But you know that if the Hulder woman appears in a red dress she is very angry, and you have to be extra careful. Singing a hymn, or saying a prayer or reciting a scripture from the Bible will keep you safe. Also carrying something made of steel makes them unable to touch you."

Listening to Lise's grandmother was both scary and exciting. When I walked from her home I kept my eyes wide open, for although I believed that the stories were probably just fairy tales or perhaps a dream, some part of me still wondered if perhaps they could be true. The people who had the ability to see *Huldra* (the Hulder) often had some special gifts of healing or insights into the future or hidden things. We said they were *"synsk."* And so I often sang softly to myself to be safe, and I had no shortage of hymns to sing.

My own mother also had a special *Huldre* story. It was something that happened to her great-grandmother. It went like this:

One night my great-grandmother had a strange dream. A beautiful and well-dressed woman came to her and said. "Why are you hurting my son?"

"How can I be hurting your son when I don't even know you?"

"You are hurting him when you place your wooden milk bowls to dry against the south wall of the house. Don't do that!"

Great-grandmother knew this was the Hulder, but she decided not to pay heed to the warning. After all she was a devout Christian lady, who believed that God was more powerful than these hidden people. So she continued to put her large, wooden milk bowls to dry in the usual place.

A couple of nights later the woman came back. This time she looked angry, and her hair was loose and unkempt.

"Didn't I warn you not to put your bowls against the south wall of the house? You are hurting my son, and I don't want you to do that. Now I am warning you again. Don't do it!"

Then she disappeared.

When great-grandmother awakened she felt uneasy, but she shook her fears off, and placed the bowls in the sun as before.

A third night the woman came back. She looked terrible. Her face was all haggard, her hair hung in wild, matted chunks, and her clothing was all torn and dirty. She held one arm behind her back. Suddenly she brought her arm forward, and by her hand she held a little boy. His face was black and blue and bloody, and there were bumps all over his head.

"See, what you have done to my son. Because of that I give you this: Twee, twee, twee!!!"

She spat on great grandmother, and the spittle landed in the left hip area of her dress. The woman and her boy became invisible again.

The next morning, when great-grandmother awakened she could not move her left leg, because her hip hurt so much, and when she looked she discovered that her hip was all black and blue. Great grandmother had to stay in bed for three days, and never again did she place her wooden milk bowls to dry on the south wall of her house.

This story has been passed on in our family, and is only one of the many, many *Huldre* stories told in Norway, especially out in the far-away valleys and countryside.

When I was a child, many older people believed that nature was full of beings we could not see, and that we must learn to live in harmony with them or we would be in trouble. But if we treated them well and with respect, they would in turn treat us well, and make our lives good and prosperous.

Lise's grandmother was a true believer in all these invisible beings.

19
Back Again to Senja

In the spring of 1941 British warships made raids on Norwegian coastal communities. They destroyed German facilities and killed German soldiers. When they left, many young Norwegians, mostly men, fled with them back to England. Papa's two youngest brothers went. The Germans arrested and took what they called *"gisler,"* who were really hostages from the Norwegian population.

March 4th, 1941, such a raid happened in Svolvær, Lofoten. When the British left they took with them 200 German soldiers as prisoners, and 10 local NS people. The repercussions were severe, and we were afraid. The Germans burned many homes, and many prisoners were sent off to the South.

Rumors were flying that Harstad would be next, so my parents decided that we should leave for a safer place. Papa was now back in Narvik, on the same ferry as before the war started. He was an engineer, and rented a room with the family of one of the other crew members.

Once more we chartered a fishing boat. Now we had furniture and more things, so all of us helped with lifting and carrying. Again we ended up on the big island of Senja, but on a different side of the island at a place called Stonglandsteidet. Here we were able to rent one half of a farm house. There was a living room and kitchen downstairs, and a couple of bedrooms upstairs for us. It was an old house, and not very clean, but Mama felt we would be safe here. It was very unlikely that there would be any raids in this isolated place.

Four persons lived in the other half of the house. They were the owners. The oldest was Ane. She was an old woman, but still capable of doing many farm chores. She had to, because her two daughters were handicapped. Othelia, whom we called Tella was blind. Still she worked like a normal person—almost. She milked the cows and goats, made cheese and butter. She washed clothes, cooked and cleaned the house. Mama asked her how she knew when things were clean. "Oh," she said, "I just keep at it long enough, until I think it is clean." She carded and spun the wool, and knitted sweaters and socks, mittens and caps and scarves. After a while I forgot that she was blind, except when she walked outside she held her hands out away from the body. She set and cleared the table, washed dishes, and to top it all she had to take care of her sister Inga who lay in bed 24 hours a day. Inga had had polio many years ago, and could do nothing for herself.

The fourth person was Tella's son Alsén who was in his late teens. He did all the hard work on the farm. He liked my sister Marit very much, and they went to dances together on Saturday nights.

Tella taught me to card the wool, first with a coarse carder, then with a fine one. When the wool was all soft and fluffy with no twists or hard places in it we shaped it into soft rolls, about the size of a banana. With the spinning wheel going, I learned to stretch the roll into yarn, It was very hard at first to keep the yarn from getting lumpy and uneven, but I soon got the hang of it, and was very proud of myself when Tella said I was a good little spinner, and made nice, even yarn. The single-strand yarn would be twisted with one or two more strands using a special tool. Finally it was wound around a three-pronged wooden arm and made into skeins.

On this farm they had white and black sheep, so we would make both kinds of yarn. Sometimes we would card them together, both black and white, and then we got gray yarn. I really liked learning all these new skills.

In Inga's room stood a pump organ, on which I picked out melodies and sang lots of songs. Inga said she enjoyed listening to me, so I spent much time in there.

Inga's body was the strangest I had seen. They said the polio had made her that way. She always lay on her back in bed. On top she was kind of fat with a round face, double chin, and big breasts that floated out sideways. Her arms had stiffened in a position with the elbows bent, and she could move her whole arm a little from side to side by moving her shoulders out and in. She always held a crumpled piece of newspaper in between her thumbs and straight, stiff fingers. She used this paper to scratch her chest, because she had sores there which she called eczema. All day long we could hear this scraping sound from her bed.

From the waist down her body narrowed, and tapered to thin, pointed feet. I thought of a mermaid when I saw her. Her whole body was stiff, like a dried fish, except for that little arm movement and a slight turning of her head from side to side.

Once a day her nephew Alsén would lift her out of bed and put her on a chair with a hole in the seat. Under the hole sat a bucket. She was supported by another chair with pillows from the chest up, in the back. Her legs stuck straight out in the air.

Inga would have to sit like that until she could produce a bowel movement. Sometimes it took a long time. She did not seem to mind that there were other people in the room, or at least I don't remember hearing anything.

When she was all done her blind sister washed her, and then Alsén put her back in bed till the next day. I felt very sorry for Inga, and spent a lot of time talking with her, and singing for her.

Inga said her eczema came because her bed was sitting under a window, and the sun would burn her. I helped put Nivea cream on her every day. Then I started getting sores and scabs between my fingers, and it itched terribly. Pretty soon my sister got it too, and she hadn't even touched Inga.

Mama took us to the doctor as soon as the day for his visit in that community arrived. He shook his head and said, "Uff da! You've got scabies. It is a very infectious disease caused by tiny mites which burrow under the skin." Mama realized that Inga was the source of that misery.

We had to put some awful smelling ointment on for several days before we could have a bath. And Mama boiled all our clothes and bed linen. Fortunately the weather was nice, so everything dried on the clotheslines pretty fast. We usually had a bath every week. It was a big job. The water had to be heated on the stove, and then we took turns in the wooden tub which also was used for washing clothes.

When the clothes hung on the lines we had to keep watching them, because the goats loved to eat clothing. We liked playing with the kids, the little goat babies.

I was not allowed to put Nivea cream on Inga's chest any more, and Mama had to explain to them why. I seem to remember that they too went through this cleansing process, but they were grumpy about it. I hope poor Inga got rid of her itching.

I have thought of her many, many times. What a boring and sad life she had. But I cannot remember that she complained or felt sorry for herself, ever.

One of Mama's brothers had drowned while fishing commercially. His widow was unable to take care of their children, so two daughters were placed with families in two different communities, both of them near us. The oldest of them, Rebekka, lived with the local merchant-farmer here at Stonglandseidet. We met her here for the first time. She was well taken care of, and treated like a daughter.

Her sister Gunhild lived about six miles away. We were told she had a harder life. When she came to visit us once, Mama lavished a lot of attention on her. She even gave her red fox fur collar to Gunhild. I always liked to wrap the red fox fur around my neck, and felt a pang of jealousy that Gunhild got it.

But Mama explained that she felt sorry for my cousin who had to fend for herself so early in life. She was probably 12 or 13 years old then. Mama said we were blessed with two parents who looked after us. That was worth much more than a red fox fur. Now Gunhild could touch the soft fur and remember that she was not completely alone, but that Tante Dagny (Mama) loved her and was thinking of her. I liked the way Mama explained things.

We never met the youngest cousin, Torbjørg. She was able to stay with her mother.

Stonglandseidet was a fairly narrow strip of land between the big island of Senja and a peninsula called Hofsøy. On one side was Tranøyfjord, on the other side Vågsfjord, which opened up into the Atlantic Ocean. Because the storms often swept hard over this piece of land, all the houses and buildings had to be anchored to the ground at the four corners with heavy chains. Even the church was in chains.

We heard stories of how a fishing boat had been tossed from Tranøyfjord half-way across the isthmus during one winter storm. Another time the storm tore off the church roof.

We were there during the spring, summer and early fall of 1941, so we did not experience any harsh weather, but the wind often blew hard enough so my sister and I could spread our arms out and give all our weight to it. It was so much fun to be completely carried by the wind. The trouble was that the gusts would suddenly end, and we would lose our balance and fall down. But even then it was fun. All in all, the months we spent at Stonglandseidet seemed a happy time.

Vesla (Kirsten) and Hanna
at Stonglandseidet

20

Going Home to Ankenes

In the early summer of 1941 Mama went to visit Papa in Narvik. The refugees had started to move back again, building new homes in place of the burned ones. Since we had been renters and not home-owners, we did not have property to build on, but the County was buying lots and setting up so-called Swedish houses. Sweden was a neutral country so the war did not affect it, and the Swedish people donated material for new homes for the Norwegian people. It came by railroad to the border, and we had to pay to have it brought the rest of the way, as well as the construction cost.

Papa was able to get the promise of one of these homes across the harbor from Narvik, in Ankenes, where we had lived before the war. He hoped the house would be ready in August so we could get back before school started.

We were very excited about moving home again. It was over a year since we had left, and so much had changed. We kept asking Mama about all the details—who lived where, who had returned, was the grocery store still there, and the church, and the school? Where exactly would we live? She did not know. The authorities had not yet decided which house would be ours. Several new areas were being developed. We just had to be patient and be glad to get a home any place.

One day we got a letter from Papa. He said he had been given a choice of two houses, and had picked one up in the hills with a very spectacular view of the fjord and the mountains. "Just wait until you see it," he said.

Facing the main road was a row of eight houses, and above them another little road with four houses. Ours would be the second to the last of these four. It had three stories, a cellar with four rooms, one for food storage, a wash room with a stove to heat water for clothes washing, a third for wood storage, and a roughed in bathroom. It even had a water closet (toilet). No more outhouses for us. On the main floor above was a small outer hall to keep the cold out, then a hallway with doors to the kitchen, the dining/family room, the parlor and down to the basement. The top floor had four bedrooms. Mama's eyes shone with happiness as she read the letter, and we could hardly contain our excitement. Where would we sleep with so many bedrooms? A brand new house, just for our family! It surely was wonderful news.

More letters followed. Some delays would keep us waiting till September. When September came we learned it would be still another month. Mama was concerned about the arrival of frost and snow. How would we get the furniture up the hills? Papa said he was sure there would be a way. He missed us every bit as much as we missed him, and was eager for us to come.

Finally, at the end of October, he arrived to take us home. Everything we owned was packed in crates and boxes. We said good bye to Ane and Tella and Inga and Alsén. That was the sad part. I felt especially sorry for Inga who was stuck in her bed forever and ever. The first part of the journey was in a rowboat. It would bring us and all our things out to the local steamship which was waiting farther out in the ocean. The evening was dark, windy and cold.

Mama never liked getting into a small boat. Her father had drowned fishing when she was eight years old. Now she was tense and full of worries. She kept telling us to be careful, to watch where we stepped, to hold on tight, and so forth. We were so happy and in such high spirits that we just laughed at her and teased her a little; not too much, only enough to make her see how silly she was.

From the little boat we entered the steamship through a big opening in the side of the ship. We needed to climb the rope ladder, which was dangling down and swinging a bit, while the rowboat was rocking on the waves. It was a little tricky, just enough to be exciting, not scary, except for Mama. She was really frightened, and almost whimpered. We shouted encouraging words to her and finally she made it onto the ship.

After the family was on board, the furniture was brought out. It took several trips for the little boat, but we did not watch all that.

The ship was spacious and full of light inside. From the outside, when we first saw it in the darkness, it looked so big and black. All the windows were covered up with black curtains because of the war. Inside it had a couple of passenger lounges, and here we settled down.

At long last the engines started up loudly. We went out on the deck and watched as the ship plowed a white path in the dark water. We were going home to Ankenes again.

After many, many hours the ship moved slowly from the fjord into the harbor, Narvik on the left, Ankenes on the right. It seemed so long since we left.

Papa had made arrangements for the ship to go to the pier at Ankenes, where it normally did not stop, so we could unload there. I was so excited! My stomach was all tight and I could barely be still. There was so much I needed to find out.

The first thing I noticed was how different a face my home community had. Only four of the old houses in our neighborhood remained. The rest had burned down, with barns and outbuildings. Two new houses stood where our ski hills used to be. The little shopping center also had two new buildings, much larger than the old ones. We looked and pointed everywhere.

In the harbor, masts and smokestacks still stuck up above the water from the battles 18 months ago. I shuddered thinking of the people who were down there, drowned. I wondered if they were skeletons now. It must be terrible to drown. I did not want to think about that. Later I would often dream that I was walking on the bottom of the harbor, seeing all the dead men and trying to rescue them. I would then wake up in a cold sweat.

The school building had been taken over by the Germans. On the side of the road where our old home had been stood long German barracks. German trucks and wagons, with those giant horses in front, stood parked at the shopping center. Ankenes was not quiet and peaceful as it was before the war started. It seemed busy and noisy to me. But it was still home. The Germans were building a bridge at the east end of the harbor to connect Ankenes and Narvik, and some day it might replace the ferry. For many years before the war, the county officials had discussed building a bridge, but the current was strong in this area, so nothing ever came of it. "Leave it to the Germans to make this project a reality," people said.

Our house was about a ten-minute walk from where we had lived before the war. Every neighborhood had its own name, even if it was a cluster of only a dozen homes. Since our house was one of 12 "Swedish" houses, our new neighborhood was called *Svenskhusene ved Kirken,* the Swedish Houses by the Church.

Papa had been able to get a small truck to take our furniture. It seemed to take too long to get it loaded, because we could not leave until all the boxes and things were on. What did not fit on the truck was loaded on a big two-wheel push-cart. We carried the small things.

Finally we were off. How fast I walked! Up the incline from the shopping center, then a long road straight ahead. Now up the long, curvy hill past the church, the white, eight-cornered church with the black roof and bell tower on top. Memories of Christmas Eve services, of flickering candles and shining faces, of organ music and singing, of the slow, heavy bells and the fast, happy bells came flooding over me as we walked past. We also walked past the barracks where guards marched back and forth outside.

Then I saw it, a rusty ship aground below the road by the church. It was the *Bockenheim*, the ship that had been burning the morning the war started. How strange to see it again. It was lying on one side with the whole broadside upturned to the street. So much had happened since that morning.

Ankenes Church pictured before the war. Narvik harbor lies behind.
The houses in the foreground were all destroyed.

And there was the new road, where our house would be. The road
was full of rocks and mud and gravel, up the hill and between the row
of houses. The truck bumped along slowly. The push-cart got stuck
several times, and our arms were tired of pushing and carrying.

Past the Pedersen house and the Radman house we saw it, our house.
It was yellow with white trim. It stood tall and rectangular on the
gray cement walls of the cellar. Three windows on each floor faced
north, the entrance door with a window above faced east. A tall cement
staircase led up to the door, without a railing. Inside the staircase
was a small storage room.

But there was no road up to the house, only a small, crooked pathway
between the jagged rocks which had been dynamited out of the
mountain side to make room for the house.

"My God, Karsten, you must have picked the worst lot of all," said Mama. "Up here in the rocks! How are we ever going to make it livable around us?" She sounded so unhappy. All the joy I had felt inside me flew out like a flock of frightened birds.

Mama did not like our new home! We had waited and waited so long for this moment, and now there was no happiness in it. Papa looked sad. "But the view!" he said. "Just wait till you see the view! And above us are no neighbors, just the heather and the birches, and think of all the song birds we will have in the summer time!" Mama did not answer. She just shook her head.

We moved up the path and into the house. It smelled of wood, so clean and new. The floors were wood, the long stairway on the left leading upstairs was wood, the kitchen, the dining/family room, and the parlor, all unpainted wood.

We went to the windows. We saw the houses below, the main road, the shoreline at the bottom. And there, far away across the water, were tree-covered hills, and beyond them the blue mountains with snow. It looked like a painting. The fjord disappeared to the left, going all the way to the Atlantic Ocean. On the right was Narvik with its tall mountain rising from the peninsula with iron ore-loading docks. Here the railroad wound its way around the peninsula on its way to Sweden. On top of this peninsula stood the hospital, the church and many homes.

Papa was right. We could certainly see a lot. It was a very grand view. Mama was right. It was a very rocky lot. But this was going to be our home, our very own home. Mama admitted that the view was lovely. She looked at Papa and smiled. Then she touched his cheek with her hand, in a sort of caressing way. The sadness went out of Papa's face. He lifted her up and turned her around, like a dance. "We are home!" he said.

Then he shouted as loud as he could: *"Nu kan dæm kyss mæ i røuva!"* "Now they can kiss my ass!" We were shocked. Papa was saying bad words!

"Karsten!" Mama said, but she did not look serious.

"Yes," he responded "Now we are free to say and do what we want. No more being quiet or scared of other people because we are depending on their charity. No more whispering and barely daring to breathe. The children can laugh and play like normal people. Yes, we are finally home. Kiss my ass, Kiss my ass, Kiss my ass!" The last he shouted again.

My little sister, my brother and I laughed like crazy, ran around, jumped and hollered like a bunch of mad children. This was the most unusual and wonderful experience our family had ever had! It was even better than Christmas, and the 17th of May, and all the birthdays put together. We were home!

The house was empty and unpainted inside. Our voices echoed through the rooms. It was a very simple house, but it was ours.

Finally we were home.

The view from our New House (photo taken 1993)

21
Knut's Birthday Party

In our new house we quickly put the furniture in place, and used three of the bedrooms for sleeping. There were no built-in closets, so the fourth bedroom became sort of a storage room for clothes and boxes, odds and ends.

Soon the window sills in the dining and living rooms were filled with flowering and green plants in white-glazed containers with gold rims. Mama liked flowers a lot. She also sewed curtains for all the windows. We felt very much at home again.

One afternoon Kirsten announced, "They are coming at 5 o'clock." We called Vesla by her real name now, since she had started first grade.

Mama looked at her. "Who are coming?"

"The children."

"What children?"

"The children for Knut's birthday party."

It was November 3rd, and our little brother turned two years old.

"Are you crazy?" Mama asked. "I don't have any plans for a party. We have barely moved in, and there is nothing available to make a cake or cookies with. I don't have anything to give them to eat. And who are the children, anyway?" My sister started to mention some names, about six to eight of them.

"And you have invited these children to a party in a couple of hours without even asking me?"

"Yes, it is Knut's birthday, and we have to have a party," said Kirsten.

Well, Mama quickly made heart shaped waffles, a pitcher of blueberry *saft* (juice diluted with water), and a platter of open faced sandwiches. Fortunately we had been able to bring some butter and cheese with us from Senja.

The children arrived and placed their shoes and overcoats in the hallway. In the living room we played song games and guessing games. Some had brought little presents, a couple of books and some wooden toys.

Knut was a good singer at two years of age, so he had to perform for us. We were so proud of him. We would take him with us to the store and set him on the counter. Then he would sing, and the people in the store would be quiet and listen. When he finished they told him what a clever boy he was. Sometimes he would get a treat. Sometimes we sisters would also be included.

One day the store owner again asked him to sing. Knut was getting a little tired of this, so he sighed, and announced, "I'll do it, but first I have to go home and shave." Everyone started laughing very loudly. This became one of the stories we told over and over again when friends came to visit and they heard him singing.

Two of the books he got for his birthday were stories about two brothers, named *Snild* and *Slem.* Those names are really Norwegian words meaning Nice and Naughty. The stories were told in verses, and could be sung to familiar melodies. We spent many hours looking at the pictures and singing these stories about the two boys who acted just the opposite of each other.

If Knut did not behave the way we thought he should we would ask him, "Who do you think you are like now?" Of course he would have to say, "Slem." Then we would ask, "But you don't want to be like him, do you?" Of course he would have to answer in the negative, and start being nice again.

In our family we did not have spankings. If we did wrong it was usually because we did not know the rules, or had not considered the consequences. Mama would talk with us and explain why we could not say or do certain things.

We were not allowed to show anger by calling each other names, or being physical, like shoving or hitting. If ever we did that, Mama would shame us, and we had to go and sit in "The Shame Corner" which was a chair away from the others. We were not allowed to speak while sitting there. This was a very painful and humiliating experience, and did not happen very often.

We were allowed to argue, even loudly for a short while, about who was right or who was wrong, but not to tease in a mean way or say bad words. Children were expected to move quietly and speak with soft voices inside the house.

Even at birthday parties these rules had to be obeyed. Children who could not do so would not be invited.

At Knut's party, when we finished eating, which was the last part, each child would curtsey or bow while shaking Mama's hand, saying: *"Takk for maten"* (Thank you for the food.)

Then they went out in the hallway, put on their shoes and coats, and left. We thought the first birthday party at our new house had been just perfect, even if it was unplanned.

22
Back To School, 1941-1942

Since the school building was occupied by German soldiers, classes were held in private homes, in offices, or wherever there were rooms large enough. My fourth grade class was split in two with the girls in one home, and the boys in another.

I was looking forward to a full school year. Second grade had ended with the coming of the war. In third grade we left in the Spring because of British raids. Now I would not have to leave anymore.

In my neighborhood, The Swedish Houses, lived four other girls in fourth grade, Synnove, Marit, Anne Marie and Greta. They had been in my first and second grade also. I walked to school with Anne Marie the next day. We became best friends for the rest of the grade school years, and have remained so ever since.

It was so exciting to be seeing again the girls I had known so long. Although it was only a year and a half since we were separated by the beginning of the war, it seemed such a long time ago. All that had happened, all the places we had been, all the people we had met made me feel like a whole life had passed since April 9th, 1940. Now it was late October, 1941.

As we walked to school Anne Marie told me many things about her life these past eighteen months. I learned where they had been and when they returned. It turned out that ours was the last family to return. A couple of families had moved to the southern part of Norway.

I felt a bit shy when we came into the classroom, but the others told me where I could sit. They said, "Welcome back," and I thought that was very nice. I felt happy.

Our teacher was a young man who lived in Narvik, and commuted on the ferry every day. We usually arrived at school before he did, so we had time to talk and discuss many things with each other early in the morning. His name was Harry Westrheim. He had a glass eye. He was not stern and remote like some of the older teachers, but seemed to understand a lot. I liked him right away. We called him Westrheim, not with a Mister in front.

There was one problem. When he spoke to one of us, it was hard to tell which one, for one eye seemed to look one way, the other eye in a different direction. We were very respectful of our teacher, and tried to not hurt his feelings about his glass eye. One day Anne Marie asked him straight out, "Are you speaking to me or to Greta?" We were shocked at her daring question, so shocked that we had to tell this incident at home.

We had six class periods each day, with a ten minute break in between. During the break we had to go outside while as many windows as possible were opened for the room to be aired out. This was also the time to use the outhouse. When we returned to the classroom we started another subject.

Every day we had a different schedule, but each week was the same for half the school year. Every grade had a certain amount of material to get through. It was the same for all the schools in Norway. It was called *Pensum* (syllabus).

We had math and Norwegian, which included writing and reading and grammar. We had history and geography, nature studies, religion, drawing and singing. I liked singing, math and Norwegian the best.

Sometimes the teacher read a short story, and afterwards we had to write it down in our own words. Sometimes we made up stories. They could be something like *The Adventures of a Dime,* or *He Who Laughs Last Laughs Best.* I also liked to write things like *My Favorite Winter Day* or *A Summer Morning In Northern Norway.*

School was wonderful. During the lunch break we quickly ate the food we had brought with us, then went out to play for about 20 minutes. We jumped rope or played a kind of baseball with just two bases. We played song games, hide and seek, or tag. In the winter we made a sliding hill and took turns on sleds or a large piece of cardboard—or even just on our shoes. We also talked a lot, and had serious discussions on the war, on books we had read, on our sisters' boy friends, and about God.

We got our grades twice a year—at Christmas and on the last day of school. They were written in one book with our name on, and took in all seven years of grade school, so we could compare from year to year, not only our grades, but the subjects. We took them home for our parents to see, and had to return them on the first day of the new year or school year.

Every child carried a briefcase to and from school. It held our text books and our writing books, one for each subject. Most of us had something called a *Penal*. It was a wooden box about 9x3x3 inches. The top portion could be opened and swung away from the bottom portion. It was divided into sections. In the bottom sections we kept pencils, a sharpener and an eraser. In the top section we had pen holders, nibs or pen points and something to wipe the nibs with. We wrote with ink which was kept in ink wells at school.

After school we walked home together in happy groups. Often we sang the new songs we had learned or discussed things we had heard. When we met German soldiers we cracked jokes about them, for we were sure they did not understand. Then we laughed uproariously. Sometimes we asked for candy, which we could no longer buy in the stores. We learned to say; *"Hast du Bon-bon?"* Sometimes they gave us some.

When we met Norwegian adults we curtseyed and said, *"Goddag!"* (good day). The boys nodded instead of curtseying. To be polite was an important part of being a child, and the grown ups always responded to our greetings.

At home dinner waited, usually some kind of fish with potatoes. Vegetables were hard to get, and not served every day. We had a couple of hours to play outside, but also quite a bit of homework.

Often I went to Anne Marie, and we studied together, especially all the memory work. During school hours we would be tested, usually verbally, one at a time, to see if we had learned our lessons. We had to stand up next to our desk while we recited our memory work or answered questions.

To do well in school was extremely important, and the highest honor was to be the best in your class. That earned respect from the other children. Unfortunately, we were not very kind to those who had a hard time learning. Often we would ignore them during recess, or just barely tolerate them.

We were 12 girls in fourth grade. Ten of us became very close. We went to each other's birthday parties, and played together during and after school. Two were left out. They were the shy and not-so-clever ones. Thinking about it now seems so cruel and unkind, but that is how we behaved. The teacher never got involved with us during recess. That was our time.

As it turned out, this school year would not be normal either.

We knew of friction between the teachers and the NS leaders. The teachers were asked to join the party, but they did not want to. Suddenly we got a month off. They called it a fuel-vacation. It was to save wood and coke or whatever was used to heat the school rooms.

A month later our teacher was arrested. Two of the teachers in our little community were. Our teacher, Harry Westrheim, was sent to a prison camp near Tromsø, further north. Over a thousand teachers were arrested in all of Norway. They were accused of being subversive, of teaching children disrespect for the NS government.

I don't remember how long he was gone, but when he came back we were not allowed to sing our national anthem, *Ja, Vi Elsker Dette Landet* (Yes, we love this land) or our national hymn, *Gud Signe Vårt Dyre Fedreland* (God bless our precious fatherland). We were also not allowed to discuss anything about the war or occupation.

One of the girls asked what it was like to be arrested, but our teacher said, "We will not talk about that."

We heard reports that some children had told their parents, who were Nazi sympathizers, about what certain teachers had said, and that is why they were put in prison. We knew that in our class we had no "spies", but still the atmosphere was changed. We could not be ourselves and be as free as we had been before in our relationship with the teacher.

I remember that he read something in front of the class the first day he was back. His lips were all dry, and he looked pale. We did not really understand the full meaning of what he said, although we understood the words.

But we did understand that he would not teach us that we should believe in NS, which we would not have done anyway.

23
The New Order and the Schools

The New Order was to be enforced on all aspects of life in Norway. This included all organizations and institutions. The Norwegians were a well-organized people. Almost every citizen was a member of some group or other, social and athletic clubs, business and professional organizations, workers' unions, women's volunteer societies, etc. Teachers, clergy, doctors and nurses, telephone and transport workers, farmers, bakers and so on were represented in close to 50 different organizations.

The newspapers reported the edicts from on high, "Every public employee must work actively for the NS party. Every institution and organization must promote the party to serve effectively the land and its people. The smallest form of failure will be regarded as an enemy action against our country. Drastic punishments will from now on be meted out to every enemy of the State."

A sharp letter of protest was delivered to Terboven May 17th, 1941. It was signed by 43 occupational organizations, representing over 750,000 countrymen, about one-fourth of the whole Norwegian citizenry. In it they said that the Nazification of Norwegian institutions, and Nazi-inspired proclamations and decisions were blatantly "contrary to law."

Terboven became furious. He announced that his patience with the Norwegians had run out. Some of the leaders were arrested. Others were warned that he would tolerate no more trouble. He dissolved several of the national organizations, and put NS members as leaders in others. These soon ceased to exist as the regular members resigned their membership *en masse*. They did however start "B" organizations, which were illegal underground groups. In time these would coalesce into an organized system of resistance against the Nazi regime.

The teachers had several groups: city teachers, country teachers, women teachers, and so forth. These were some of the 43 that sent the protest letter. But they had been under pressure earlier. Shortly after Terboven's speech September 25th, 1940, a few of the more eager NS members went to local school boards and gave teachers the ultimatum to become members of the party or be fired. By the end of October the teacher organizations sent out a letter to their members saying that this pressure did *not* come from the Department of Church and Education, but from local officials. Joining a political party or not had always been a voluntary decision, and this kind of pressure should not be tolerated. It also referred to the Hague Convention and international law.

A month later the Department issued a letter to the teachers: "As is obvious to all, the Norwegian people are now facing a profound political, social and cultural New Order." The letter spelled out the teachers' responsibility to actively educate the children in this New Order, and declare that they would be willing to do so. If not they would be fired.

The teachers immediately responded, "I declare that I will be true to my calling and to my conscience, and that I will in the future as in the past follow the instructions given to me by my legitimate superiors."

NS officials tried to pressure single districts and teachers, but were not successful, as the students themselves made very clear where their loyalty was. A breathing space in the struggle followed.

Then came another memorable day in occupation history. On February 1st, 1942 at an official gathering at Akershus Castle, Vidkun Quisling was made Minister-president of Norway.

He was given a chance to really prove that he could turn Norway into a national socialistic country. But Terboven and the *Reichskommisariat* remained in the country.

Two days later Quisling sent out a proclamation that all boys and girls between 10 and 18 years should join the NS Youth Movement,

NSUF. This meant that they would be forced to march under the old Viking symbol, the yellow and red sun-cross, sing NS songs, be subjected to NS propaganda, and cultivate sports and activities under the leadership of *Hird* (Norwegian Nazi) youth.

Another two days, and Quisling decided that all occupations should be joined into NS unions with compulsory membership.

It took a week for a combined group of teachers from elementary and high schools to create a letter which each individual teacher was to send to the Department of Church and Education: "I find that I cannot cooperate in raising Norway's youth after the guidelines made for NSUF as it is against my conscience. As membership in the new teachers' union obliges me to do so, and also other activities which are contrary to my employment contract, I need to inform you that I do not regard myself as a member of the New Order teacher union."

Ragnar Skancke, the Minister of Education, replied that he considered the refusal of the teachers equivalent to their resignation. Therefore, they would suffer loss of pay and denial of pension benefits.

Undeterred, 98 per cent of the teachers remained solidly against these threats. They decided they would do nothing except continue teaching until they were fired, one by one.

Intellectually and morally helpless against this wall, the government found itself in a deep dilemma. What to do? The schools could not continue without teachers. The order could not be relaxed.

Minister-president Quisling resolved the embarrassment by ordering that all schools be closed for a month. "Because the severe winter this year has severely reduced the country's heating resources we have decided that from February 27th there will be one month's Fuel Vacation from all elementary and high schools." This obvious attempt at saving face became the subject of more jokes and contempt.

At the same time the Department showed its "consideration" by giving the teachers another month's deadline.

Now it was as if an avalanche had rolled over Norway. The resistance from the Church and School had served to unify the country even more against NS. An illegal pamphlet was copied and recopied and passed to every home throughout the country. The parents were to send the following to the Department, signed with full name and address, "I do not wish for my children to be part of NSUF's youth service, as the guidelines for this work is against my conscience."

Sacks and sacks of this letter poured in to the Department in early March. When the teachers' month of consideration was up there was no change. Terboven was both satisfied and worried. His warnings that Quisling could not deliver had come true. At the same time the occupation forces' prestige had been damaged as the Allied propaganda made the most of this Norwegian civil disobedience. He had the ultimate power and responsibility for the situation in Norway.

Mid-March he called Quisling to his office. They agreed that a thousand teachers should be arrested and sent to labor camps in North Norway. March 20 saw eleven hundred teachers arrested. About five hundred were sent on a small ship with 96 passenger capacity from Trondheim, heading north. Rumors were that the Germans would sink the ship, and blame the British. There was of course the danger of mines and torpedoes. Several ships had gone down along the coast with the loss of many civilians. The biggest one-time loss was when the coastal steamer *Barøy* was sunk, December 9th, 1941. Thirty or more persons just from Narvik perished. Many were University students going home for Christmas.

The five hundred teachers had a terrible trip, packed like slaves and treated as such. The others were sent to other prison camps. Many went to Grini, near Oslo, where some of the priests and other leading Norwegians were imprisoned.

Kirkenes is as far north and east as it is possible to go in Norway. Here the five hundred suffered a great deal. They had horrible living quarters, hard labor, poor food and little of it. Their clothes and shoes wore out. The weather was awful. They were wet and cold all the time. Some became ill and were told that they would be allowed to go home if they signed the declaration. The teachers discussed this. They knew they could not stay alive if they remained there. All the teachers agreed to sign. "I declare that I am a member of the teachers' union, and after full recovery I will resume my work under the resolutions in force."

Little by little they returned, the last ones not until November. In the meantime some schools started again in April with non-arrested and substitute teachers. Later that same month the Department wrote that teachers would not be assigned any new duties that were contrary to their contracts. But they were automatically members of the teachers' union as long as they taught.

On the first day back at school the teachers read a declaration in front of the class stating that teaching and union membership were two different things. As teachers they were not only to dispense knowledge and training, but to teach their students to believe in and to will what is good and true and just. "I will therefore never teach anything that is against my conscience."

NS believed they had won the battle against the teachers. Instead, from the teachers' union came one of the most active resistance groups in Norway. It contributed financially to the "home front," and provided some of the most active leaders of the Underground. It set up an illegal fund to help the families when teachers were arrested or fired. It held conferences to discuss how to respond when the pressure on single schools and individual teachers became especially difficult.

NS had infiltrated every part of the school system, from school boards and supervisory positions to councils of education which decided what educational material was to be used. They controlled the teacher training colleges and tried in every way to impose the New Order. Yet they were never able to Nazify Norway. The schools and the churches provided the firm backbone to resist, and guided the parent organizations in how to preserve the children. It was a spiritual battle for Norway's soul which the Nazis could never win.

24

The Church and the Nazis

Arne Fjellbu was the Dean of *Nidarosdomen*, the Norman Gothic cathedral built in Trondheim around the year 1100. He had served as a pastor in Berlin during and after World War I, and had been instrumental in bringing starving German children to Norway after that war. He had also served there as a correspondent for a Norwegian paper in the 30's, so he was very familiar with Hitler's rise.

Shortly after Trondheim was occupied, he met and talked with the German commandant there. Dean Fjellbu told the German that National Socialism is irreconcilable with Christianity.

In NS the State has total control of man. Such control should only be ascribed to God.

The German remarked that he would be expected to say something like that as a pastor. "No, Captain", replied Fjellbu, "not as a pastor but as a Christian." This apparently impressed the German.

Later during the occupation Terboven and Himmler, the *Reichsfuhrer* of the SS *(Gestapo)* came to see the cathedral. Dean Fjellbu told them that the cathedral's history symbolizes the history of the country.

The Norwegian people are a religious people. Norway is a Christian nation. "The national monument of Norway is *Nidarosdomen*. Therefore the Norwegian people and the Norwegian Church are woven together. I know of no other country where this is so true. They cannot be separated."

Already during the summer of 1940, the newspapers carried an appeal from the Church to "repentance and prayer during this fateful hour."

It was not enough for Terboven to delete the church prayer for the King and his house. He also told the pastors that it was illegal to maintain "the silence of confession."

The Churches formed a coalition which they called *Kirkens Samråd.* It had many meetings.

On January 15th, 1941, the Church, through its bishops, sent a letter to the head of the Department of Church and Education. It was a protest letter regarding the confessional order, the pressure on people's conscience, the force and violence of the *Hird,* and the transgression of the laws our country was built upon. They gave well-documented examples of terror by Gestapo agents, torture and beatings, as well as the violence by Quisling's youth organization.

All the churches of Norway, both the Lutheran State churches and the independent denominations fully supported this statement.

When the response to this letter proved unsatisfactory, it was printed and sent out in a *hyrdebrev* (pastoral letter) to be read in all the churches during the worship service.

Fifty thousand copies were made. German authorities confiscated twenty thousand and prohibited the reading of it, but thirty thousand were distributed, starting February 6th.

Many of the churches disobeyed the order and read the letter. Others proclaimed, "Today a pastoral letter from the Bishops of Norway's churches should have been read, but the police have confiscated the letter, and forbidden the reading thereof."

They needed say no more. Now the conflict between the Church and the Nazi state was out in the open.

Nazification of the church had already started, but only a few Nazi pastors conducted services—for empty churches. The loyal pastors filled their churches, meeting places and even private homes.

In July, Berlin ordered that all Norwegian church bells should be made into cannons. Norway's highest bishop, Berggrav, was notified by Terboven himself. He refused this order, both verbally and by letter, warning that there would be a drastic reaction from the Norwegian people should this take place.

The matter was dropped. But the conflict continued. Arrests of pastors started in Spring, 1941.

When Quisling was appointed Ministerpresident April 1st, 1942, he became, according to NS understanding, head of both State and Church.

In Trondheim Dean Fjellbu had already announced that he himself wanted to do the high mass that day. This was before he knew of Quisling's appointment. According to church tradition and Norwegian law, that right could not be taken from him.

But the Department of Church and Education decided a Nazi pastor should do a special celebration mass that morning. He did and only a handful of people attended.

In the meantime the Dean announced that since he could not do the morning mass he would conduct a regular high mass at 2 p.m. that day. As soon as the Nazi service was over, people started streaming into the cathedral. By 1 p.m. the church was filling. At 1:25 the police came and closed the doors so no more could enter.

Fjellbu avoided arrest by staying in an adjacent office all morning and slipping into the *Domkirken* the back way. At 2 p.m. he conducted the service.

Outside at least two thousand people had gathered. It was bitterly cold, about 15 degrees below zero, but they stood. Soon they began singing Luther's hymn, *A Mighty Fortress Is Our God.* Then followed the national hymn and the national anthem. After the singing they quietly left and went home.

Fjellbu was immediately removed from office. Norway's seven bishops resigned. They stated in their letter that they resigned only from their State office, not from their position as spiritual leaders, which had been conferred upon them by ordination at God's altar.

On Easter Day, April 5th, a letter called "The Foundation of the Church" was read in all the churches. It asserted that the Church was independent of the State in spiritual matters. "You must obey God rather than man." The Word of God was above all ideologies. It was really a statement of belief, contained in six articles:

- About the Word of God and our duty based on it.
- About the Church and ordination of pastors.
- About the sacred community in the Church.
- About the parents' and Church's right and duty in the bringing up of children.
- About the right relationship of the Christian and the Church to government.
- About the State Church.

After reading this, 645 of the country's 699 pastors resigned from their government positions. They continued their services and the local parishes supported them financially during the rest of the occupation years.

On April 8th, the Department sent a letter to all those pastors who had been State employees, telling them events would take place in a few days which ought to influence their decision. It referred to previous Quisling announcements that to resign State offices in protest would be "an act of rebellion directed at Norway's freedom and independence." The punishment was long imprisonment, which meant being sent to German prison camps, or death.

Quisling gave them to April 14th at 2 p.m. to withdraw their resignation by telegram. Only two telegrams arrived. Everyone thought that now some pastors would be executed as a lesson, but nothing further happened. The pastors continued ministering to the people even after their robes were taken away.

The Bishops established a Temporary Church Leadership, DMK, which in reality meant that the regular pastors and church boards still functioned, but not as part of the State. We now had two Churches in Norway, the Nazi state church and the traditional original Norwegian Lutheran Church.

When the persecution of the Jews started in the fall of 1942, DMK sent strong letters of protest to Quisling saying that this was not only against the Biblical commandment to love your neighbor, but also against the most basic human rights. "The foundation of Christianity which you have promised to uphold is being removed."

There was no reply.

Norway had about eighteen hundred Jews in 1940. After the war only twelve returned. The rest were executed or presumed perished in German concentration camps.

By the end of the war many churches had been robbed of beautiful art objects, and forty church buildings were in ruins. All the bishops had been fired, many arrested, deported or silenced in other ways. All the seminaries had been closed. Many pastors were also arrested. Two died in concentration camps.

At the end of the war there were still thirty-five pastors in prison or concentration camps. But the church built of living stones had survived, and was more alive than ever.

25
Anne Marie's Brother Nils

My best friend, Anne Marie had only one sibling. His name was Nils. He was about two years younger than we were. I did not like him because once he caught a fly and pulled its wings off while the fly was still alive. Then he laughed. Another time he showed us some tiny baby birds without feathers. Their skin was pink and their eyes covered with a thin membrane. When we asked where he got them, he just laughed again. I thought he was a bad boy.

One spring day I went to the store for my mother to find out if we would get any milk that day. During the war milk was rationed, and some days only children under six years of age and sick people would get a half-liter, other days children under fourteen would get a quarter-liter, so we never knew how much milk we could buy each day. The milk arrived every day on the ferry from the dairy in Narvik, and was sold in the grocery store here in Ankenes, across the harbor.

As I waited in line, a young boy came running into the store. He shouted, "Nils fell into the water." Many people rushed out onto the pier, and there he was, floating face down a little way out. A couple of men ran down some stairs, and tried to reach him, but they could not. After a while a young man who knew how to swim jumped in and got hold of him. He carried him on his shoulders like a sack of potatoes out of the water, onto the beach. Nils' arms and legs were limp, and sort of slapping the young man's back with each step he took. Water was running from both of them.

They placed Nils face down and started doing Holger Nielsen's maneuver. I had learned that. You lift the arms above the head, then bring them down again and press on the rib cage, over and over again. This was supposed to bring air into and out of the lungs. They kept doing that a long time. A big crowd had gathered around and was silently watching.

Suddenly we heard a loud wail up the road. A woman came bicycling very fast down towards us, screaming. She jumped off the bike before it even stopped. The bike crashed to the ground with its wheels still spinning. She pushed her way through the crowd and fell down next to Nils. It was his mother. She wailed and sobbed and cried out loud, without any control.

I was stunned. Where I grew up people did not act that way. They carried their grief inside, very quietly. It was all right to wipe your tears, and blow your nose, but you did not make such a racket, no matter how distraught you were.

I thought she looked like a crazy, wild person and it scared me. I had always known her as an ordinary, regular mama who spoke softly like most mothers did, smiled often and was very kind. Now she was completely different, and I felt frightened.

After a while people started saying, "It is no use. He is dead. Nils is dead." The crowd began dispersing. We walked quietly and somberly back to the store. Our voices were almost like whispers. Nils is dead. Nils drowned.

I walked home as fast as I could to tell my mother. Her eyes became big, and she said, "Oh no, what are you saying? How did it happen?" Over and over I told the story, to her, to my sisters and brother, to everyone who did not know. It was such a terrible thing. My best friend's brother was dead, and I had not even liked him. I felt very bad. Dying at 9 years of age was very horrible.

Anne Marie, did not come to school the next day or the day after. When I passed her house I felt shy if I saw her outside. I said *"Hei,"* and she said *"Hei,"* but I did not know what else to say.

The funeral was in their front yard. Nils, dressed in a white *lik skjorte* (shroud), was lying in a white casket. It was the first time I saw someone who was dead. He looked asleep, but his face was yellow-white. His hands were folded over his chest, and his fingers were bluish-black. A small, black hymn book was under his hands.

The pastor wore a long black robe with a piped, stiff white collar. He spoke in a low, serious voice. We sang hymns. I felt so sad that the tears just kept coming.

I looked at Anne Marie. She had on a navy-blue sailor suit with a pleated skirt. She looked so nice. Her brown eyes were very dark. She just stared straight ahead. Her mother no longer wailed. She just cried and cried, sometimes a little bit loud, but also quietly. Her father cried too. His face became all screwed up and funny looking. I almost wanted to laugh, but it would have been terrible to laugh at a funeral. I did not look at him again.

They closed the lid and placed many floral wreaths on the casket. There was one from our school. We all had contributed money. The casket was lifted onto the back of a truck and people climbed up and crowded around it. There was also a second truck for carrying people on the long, slow ride out to the cemetery, seven or eight kilometers away. All along the route, at almost every house, a Norwegian flag was flown at half-mast on a tall white flag pole. It may not have been legal, but they still did it. When we passed people on the road, they would stop. The men would take their caps or hats off until we passed. The trucks drove so slowly that those who could not get on them could walk behind. We took turns sitting and walking. It was more than an hour to the cemetery.

Finally we came to this very soundless place in the pine forest. We never talked loudly at the cemetery, only very gently, and we walked slowly and softly too. All around were gravestones of hundreds of people. Some I had known, some had died a long time ago. My own baby brother was buried there. For many years he was an unseen presence in my life.

Soon after we returned to Ankenes I had asked Mama where he lay buried. She told me the approximate place. I borrowed a bicycle and rode out to the cemetery. I looked at many, many graves, and then I found it—an old, weather-beaten wooden cross which had been white a long time ago. His name could be seen carved into it. He had my father's and grandfather's name, Karsten Leonard. I cleaned up all the weeds, found an empty tin behind the tool shed, and picked some wildflowers. These I placed on his grave, and sang our special song. It made me cry. It seemed to me that I finally was able to really say good bye to him then, all alone in that still and solemn place.

A grave had been dug for Nils in the gray-brown sandy earth. Three wooden boards were lain across, and here they placed Nils' casket. The pastor read from the Bible. We sang another hymn. It was hard to sing—our voices became sort of shaky with sadness. As they lowered the flower-decked casket into the ground, a great stillness rested over us. Then Nils' mother started to cry again, very loudly. My own chest felt tight and I felt it was almost difficult to breathe.

The pastor took earth in his hand and said, "From earth you are taken, to earth you shall return, and from earth you shall rise again." With every sentence he tossed a little of the earth on the casket. It made a sound like rain falling. We sang another hymn and prayed. Slowly we turned from the grave and walked back to the trucks. Now all the people were packed onto them for the ride home at normal speed.

At Nils' home long tables had been set, and even though it was wartime and difficult to get food, there were heart waffles and open-faced sandwiches, "coffee" made of roasted barley for the grownups, and *saft* for the children. We tried to say nice things about Nils. I smiled at Anne Marie and she smiled at me.

The next day she was back in school, and life gradually became normal again. But her mother kept crying so much that she had to put yellow ointment on her eyes all the time. It took a long time before she stopped crying.

Anne Marie and I became even closer friends, since we now both had brothers at the cemetery. Sometimes we would walk to the cemetery and visit their graves together. She is still my friend.

A year or two later Anne Marie got a little baby brother. His name was Nils.

26
Konzentrationslager 1. Narvik-Beisfjord

Southeast of Narvik, where the harbor continues into a narrow fjord, lies Beisfjord. Right in the middle of this little community, on a small plain surrounded by steep slopes with short birch trees and the river below, was a prison camp. It had twenty-seven or twenty-eight barracks. The camp was fenced in with two rows of eighteen-foot tall barbed wire. Between the fences, bundles of more barbed wire were spread out.

Above the main entrance was a sign: *Mit fleissig Arbeit-Weg in Freiheit* (with diligent work a way to freedom).

On June 24th, 1942, nine hundred Yugoslavian prisoners arrived on the ship *Kerkplein* after a long, tortuous trip from the Polish port of Sczcecin. They were weak, sick and exhausted, but were forced to walk the ten kilometers from Narvik to Beisfjord. Some of them could barely stand upright and were supported or carried by their comrades.

An old man crawled on his hands and knees and was brutally beaten by the German and Norwegian SS guards. An officer, running from one of the houses by the road, stopped it by shouting, *"Er ist krank!"* (He is sick!) The *Gestapo* heaved the old man onto the bed of a truck that had just arrived.

The guards spurred the prisonors on with long, wooden sticks, with iron spikes, or with the bayonets attached to their rifles. They sometimes even pelted the prisoners with rocks. The long road had just been covered with new gravel, hard and sharp, and the prisoners' footwear was inadequate to say the least.

After their arrival, small groups were set to work on the roads or on the piers in Narvik. They were so weak that they could not work very hard or move very fast, but the guards continued to shout at and tyrannize them.

As much as possible the civilian population tried to help with food, knitted socks and mittens which were hastily thrown to them when the guards were not looking. Some guards were more humane and looked another way. The Norwegian *Hirdmen* were often worse than the Germans.

The dying started. The Yugoslavs themselves had to dig big holes and dump the corpses in them. By July the official camp report was: Total number of prisoners: 876. Healthy: 566, Sick: 310.

On July 14th the prisoners were not called out for work. Normally they had to line up at 5 a.m. and stand outside, without shirts, for roll call. Sometimes they stood for hours before it finally pleased the guards to come and do the inventory. Northern Norway is not a warm place, even on summer mornings, and the prisoners suffered a great deal from the cold.

But this July morning there was no roll call. Instead, rolls of barbed wire were placed between the barracks of the sick and the healthy ones. The camp was divided in two.

The camp physician, Herr Doktor Grohne, announced that typhoid fever had broken out, and the whole sick camp would be quarantined for 45 days. There would be no passage between the two camps. The food would be passed through the barbed wire fence. No caregivers or any other healthy person was allowed to enter the quarantined area. Anyone trying to do so would be shot.

Some prisoners were put to work digging a big ditch. At the same time the camp's surroundings were spruced up. *Reichskommissar* Terboven would be visiting.

The ditch-digging did not proceed fast enough so some prisoners with dysentery or less serious illnesses were also forced to dig. Three ditches had been completed by July 17th. When Terboven and his group of high officers arrived, they did not enter the camp, but stood a long time outside, talking.

After they left, the prisoners began to suspect what would happen. A nervous stillness spread through the camp.

Now they discovered that the new barbed wire created a passage that led from the sick barracks to the ditches, and that the ditches were surrounded by the same wire.

All the barrack windows were covered with shutters. In the afternoon the healthy prisoners were ordered to be ready to leave by 9:00 p.m. Four groups totaling 430 prisoners left. Then another group of 155 also left. The other 287 remained behind in the sick barracks.

The executions started at 10:00 p.m. They were witnessed by several Norwegian neighbors, who had been ordered to shutter their windows and stay inside their houses that day. In the forenoon the order came that anyone disobeying would be shot.

But some young men sneaked out and hid among the trees. Others looked through small gaps in the windows or tiny openings in the attic walls. Most could not bear to watch for very long.

The prisoners were brought out about twenty at a time. They were lined up along the ditches.

After each automatic-weapon volley, two German officers walked along the ditch and finished off the ones who were still alive.

Finally no more prisoners came out. The machine guns started again, this time inside the barracks. Some of the condemned had tried to run to empty barracks, or hide under the barracks, but all were doomed.

The Germans poured a white liquid over the dead in the ditches. Then they formed a ring around the barracks. Suddenly a fire broke out. It grew bigger and bigger. Two of the barracks became infernos.

More shots were heard. Apparently they had found some people still alive, trying to escape.

When the fire burned down, a great stillness prevailed. The smell of burned wood and human flesh mingled with the smoke that drifted over Beisfjord for days.

The other Yugoslavs were sent into the mountains to work on the road being built from Narvik to Sweden. Of the 585 who left Beisfjord, 346 returned on August 25th. The rest died or were shot "because they were unable to work."

The final count of Beisfjord camp survivors was 151. They were sent to another camp in October, 1942.

Later the camp was rebuilt to house Russian prisoners of war. These prisoners were guarded by *Die Wehrmacht,* not by SS. They were treated more humanely.

All in all there were 150 prison camps in Northern Norway. By the end of the war the area held 16,400 prisoners of war. During 1944 when *Die Wehrmacht* was put in charge, the conditions improved. Then the Red Cross was able to step in and exert some influence.

After the war seventeen German guards in these camps were condemned to death by Yugoslavian and Russian courts. None of the Norwegian guards got the death penalty.

27

Norwegian Resistance

General Otto Ruge took over as Commander-in-Chief of the Norwegian forces April 11th, 1940. Two months later, on June 9th, it was his bitter duty to contact the German High Command to request an armistice. By choosing to remain with his forces rather than leave with the King and Government two days earlier, he risked imprisonment, and possibly worse. The general was indeed taken prisoner and sent first to Grini, near Oslo, then to Germany where he distinguished himself with his quiet dignity and proud bearing in spite of the harsh life in prison camps.

Before he left his troops he spoke to them. "A free man can never be conquered if he knows that within himself. So wait, believe and be prepared, each in his own community."

After surviving the first shock of war and capitulation, local groups of soldiers started to act. They began to collect ammunition, explosives and equipment. They gathered together and hid whatever arms were recovered from the fighting. Then they began to focus on how to convert the strong feelings of resistance against the Germans and Quisling's Nazi party into some kind of action. From all of Norway's occupational organizations emerged, little by little, a brotherhood with political functions. The move into the Underground took place after the protest letter of May 17th, 1941 resulted in arrests and executions.

Members were selected and recruited very carefully. Friend engaged friend. Those easily swayed, or with loose tongues, or the naïve were avoided. What social position they held, or what pre-war party they had been affiliated with, was of no importance. The qualities that counted were courage, wisdom, knowledge, discretion, resourcefulness, and above all faith in the freedom cause. They had to be people with contacts and influence. They also had to be able to communicate well to produce practical and effective results.

These small cells of patriots sprang up everywhere. No higher authority forced or even suggested that they form. Concerned and angered citizens felt they needed to do something. Our national existence was threatened, as were the values we held high: rule of law, intellectual and spiritual freedom, our special cultural heritage, all those aspects of life which made it worthwhile.

Eventually these groups became organized with a central leadership. It came about because they sought counsel from the previous intellectual, spiritual and political leaders of the land when they were uncertain on how to proceed. The first attempt to form a centrally-led, country-wide resistance group resulted in the *R-Gruppe,* short for Counsel group in Norwegian. This developed into a two-pronged leadership. One was *Kretsen (*the circle), formed mainly of Supreme Court judges, the Administrative Council and the Labor Union. *Kretsen* was primarily the civil representative to the exiled government. The other group was KK (coordination committee), which were the leaders of all the occupational organizations.

By the winter of 1941-42 the Resistance movement in Norway had become organized into two major parts: First, a coordinated, unified civilian branch of individual groups called *Civorg.* Second, a coordinated, highly centralized military organization, *Milorg*, also referred to as the 4th arm of defense.

At the same time, the exiled government in London was figuring out how to keep their promise to continue the fight outside the country's borders. They knew it would have to be as part of the Allied war against the Axis. The outlook was not rosy. But Norway had some valuable assets abroad. First, it had a large merchant fleet. Already the day after the German invasion Quisling requested that all captains of Norwegian vessels abroad were to proceed to Norwegian, German or neutral harbors immediately. Not one of those outside the reach of the Germans complied. At that time Norway ranked fourth among the shipping nations. The fleet was modern and the ships fast. One-fifth of the world's tankers were Norwegian.

During April and May 1940 Norwegian ship owners and the government in London started to organize the Norwegian Shipping and Trade mission, known as *Nortraship*. It was biggest in the world at the beginning of the war, and biggest at the end, although half the tonnage had been lost. It started with over a thousand ships and lost 550. With those ships four thousand men and women went down.

Many books have been written about the valuable contribution these sailors and ships provided, transporting supplies for the Allied war efforts, and the dangers and stresses they were subjected to constantly. The Murmansk convoys were especially harrowing, often fatal, expeditions.

Papa's two younger brothers, who fled to England from Lofoten, sailed throughout the war. One was torpedoed and rescued twice, the other took part in the Normandy landings. Almost every Norwegian family had loved ones involved in the war.

In addition to the merchant marine, the Norwegian government in London wanted to establish armed forces to assist in the war effort, but especially to be an important part of the eventual liberation force in Norway itself. From 1940 to 1945, the Royal Norwegian Navy had a total of 118 naval vessels sailing under the Norwegian flag.

In Toronto, Canada, an air force training center called Little Norway was established. It sent out four Norwegian fighter squadrons which shared fully with the Allies in establishing air superiority over southern England and the Channel, in convoy duty and anti-submarine patrols in the North Atlantic, and in frequent operations over Norway. The last included bombing raids and especially, air drops of people and equipment for the Underground.

In Scotland, an army training camp was set up, but the army received a low priority. By 1943 it had twenty-five hundred men, most of them stationed in Scotland as part of the British Isles' home defense, but also preparing for the expected war of liberation of Norway. Some of these served in a special company for secret operations in Norway.

It took awhile before the details of Norwegian-Allies cooperation were worked out. The March, 1941 Lofoten raid, the first of a series of "hit and run" raids was a British-directed operation. It led to serious repercussions in the local population. The Norwegian government demanded and got a larger input in the planning of such operations. The Norwegian High Command was established in London. Together with the British Special Operations Executive, or SOE (and later with the American Office of Strategic Services, the OSS) the planning and execution of sabotage and other secret operations in Norway were coordinated with *Milorg*.

The aim of the sabotage was to attack and cripple important targets for the German war machine: fuel, oil, gasoline, airplane engines and locomotives. It went after *Wehrmacht* camps, airfields, installations connected with transport and communication, shipping and ship building, road transport, railways and electric power. Other targets were tunnels and bridges, telephone and telegraph lines.

Important also was the destruction of Nazi archives, such as those intended to induct young Norwegians into forced German military service. In May, 1944, preparations for this was at a feverish pitch. Saboteurs entered the building full of workers scrambling to get ready for the next day's conscription start. They placed the bomb with a two-minute fuse, announced loudly that the building would blow up in a few seconds and all who wanted to were welcome to get out with them. They then tore down the stairs with all the workers in headlong rush behind them. The files were destroyed. The conscription stopped.

Civorg, the other resistance branch, printed and distributed illegal newspapers and literature. The story of the Underground press alone is an unbelievably exciting and bittersweet chapter of the resistance story. More than 325 different illegal press operations have been documented. Not only did they write and make stenciled copies by the tens of thousands, a feat in itself considering that paper was strictly rationed and controlled, but they made false passports, travel documents and legitimate papers. They had a special secret delivery system, which saw that the news was passed around but also served as a warning system to those who were at risk of being arrested, and needed to go under cover. They provided ration cards and food, and connected the various resistance groups inside the country with authorities abroad. They helped arrange meeting places and hiding places, as well as radios and weapons, for many of the press people were also members of other resistance groups. They sent out *"paroles"* (messages or instructions) which were intended to foster opposition to Nazification and recommend countermeasures to Nazi propaganda.

The secret press received many hard blows, for the *Gestapo* was especially keen to eradicate it and tried in many ways to infiltrate and "unroll" the members in these groups.

In the fall of 1941, summer and fall of 1943 and especially the spring of 1944 they suffered severe losses. But regardless of imprisonment, concentration camps and executions, new people stepped in and continued this very important work.

As the *Gestapo* sought to infiltrate the resistance groups, so the *Gestapo* was also infiltrated. Underground agents worked in the *Gestapo* headquarters at Victoria Terrasse in Oslo. They were placed at Terboven's *Reichskommisariat,* and were able to listen in on telephone conversations and intercept mail and telegraph services directed to all the important officials of *Die Wehrmacht* and NS.

The Home Front was subordinated to the authority of the King and Government in London through the Norwegian High Command. Couriers and radio messages passed between Norway and England continuously. Fishing boats left the Norwegian coast with resistance members on the run and with intelligence information. They returned with instructors, secret agents, radios, weapons, and other supplies.

One of these regular runs became known as "The Shetland Bus." They knew that capture meant death, for paragraph 2 of Terboven's edict of September 26th, 1941 said, "Anyone who tries to leave Norwegian territory, by land or by sea, must count on getting caught, and forfeiting his life."

In spite of this one of the Underground men, Captain Holst of Norway, reported to London in October, 1941, "We have 20 thousand men who are willing to risk their lives, property and personal freedom for the cause they cherish. And this number will increase."

As the German surveillance of the coast increased, the connection went east instead, over the Swedish border. Stockholm, the capital, became more and more the center for transmitting messages and intelligence reports such as maps and German documents. Special guides brought those in danger of imminent arrest on risky, tense night journeys across the heavily guarded border. Health camps had been set up in Sweden, but basic military training was given there to form Norwegian police reserves. In fact, refugees became regular army units.

In Norway there also was a military espionage network, known as XU (X for mathematical unknown, U for unknown). This was so secret that members did not know each other by sight or real name, they went by cover names. XU reported to the British Secret Information Service, SIS. Finally, there was the SG, or security guard. This group protected Underground operations against infiltration and discovery and conducted military and industrial sabotage.

The King and Government in exile were strongly connected to the home front. They provided the inspiration for the continued fight and kept alive the hope that one day Norway would again be a free and independent nation.

28
Ingebjørg Disappears

In the Fall of 1942 my oldest sister Ingebjørg disappeared. She had been working here and there, and also had a friend on an island whom she often visited. She did not really live at home, but came to visit. Sometimes she went out evenings, but she would not say where.

When she had not come home for several weeks, Mama started to worry again. One time she said, "I wonder if Bjørg was involved in something illegal." Then she really worried. We had heard of *"Nacht und Nebel"* (night and fog). Sometimes people would be taken by the *Gestapo* and never be heard of again. It was as if they had disappeared into the night and fog. Could this have happened to our sister? Or had she perhaps fled to Sweden as so many others had? They usually went during the dark time of the year so they could ski across the mountains undetected.

All along the border the Germans kept guards and bloodhounds. Anyone caught fleeing would be shot, so it was a very risky business, trying to flee.

Mama worried terribly about her. We thought she must have gone, but were not sure. Even if it were true, had she made it safely? It would take a couple of days of continuous walking to get there. First you had to climb the mountains from the Norwegian side, then ski across the mountain plateaus, and finally get down to populated areas on the Swedish side.

One day a young Norwegian Nazi came to our house. We had been warned beforehand so Mama told us that we must not speak. If we were asked questions we must just say that we did not know anything.

We were very nervous, for it happened that if a Norwegian had fled to Sweden or England, other family members still in Norway were arrested and sent off to labor camps in Germany. Sometimes the Nazis would punish the family by taking away furniture or valuables.

We sat in the kitchen, all of us, when he knocked on the door. He was dressed in the black *Hird* uniform.

We had to tell our names and ages, and he wrote it all up in a big, black book. Then he started to ask Mama all kinds of questions. When was the last time we had seen Bjørg? Had she ever mentioned whether she was part of the Norwegian Underground or resistance movement? Where did she work? Who were her friends? Lots and lots of questions. A couple of times he tried to trip Mama up by misquoting her. But Mama was always able to respond, "No, I did not say that. This is what I said."

He asked us questions too, but we just confirmed what Mama had said or said we did not know. He finally left, saying that we might hear from him again.

We were completely quiet until we knew he had gone down the hill, away from our home. Then we breathed out. Mama hoped he was satisfied and that this was the end of it.

We never heard from him again, but we learned later that he had died in an explosion. It was rumored to be the work of the Underground. This man was an informer and dangerous, they said.

All of us continued to wonder if Bjørg was safe. Mama would often sit very still with her hands in her lap. Her eyes had a far-away look. Then we knew she was thinking of our oldest sister.

One day many months later, we got a letter from Sweden. It was from Maj Magnusson, a woman we did not know at all, but the handwriting was my sister's. This Maj pretended to be a Swedish girl, but she wrote in such a way that we knew it was Bjørg telling about her life. We were so happy, for now we knew that our sister had made it safely to Sweden and we didn't need to worry about her any more, only miss her.

We learned later that she and another woman who both had been in the Underground had taken the train to the last Norwegian station before the border. They had pretended to be the girlfriends of German soldiers. At a house there they met a Norwegian guide who provided them with food, compass and maps, and brought them as far as he could towards the border. After that they were on their own.

They had been seen by German guards who set out after them, but a snowstorm came and covered their tracks. My sister did not want to talk about this, but little by little we learned a few details. The other woman had become exhausted and wanted to lie down in the snow, so Bjørg had to beat her with the ski poles to keep her going.

They were very cold and very hungry and at the end of their strength when they reached the first Swedish house. Here they were taken in and given food and rest.

A network of assistance had been established in Sweden for refugees. They were able to find work and friends among the other refugees, and among the Swedes.

After the war my sister eventually returned to Sweden, went to school there, and became a registered nurse with specialties in surgery, obstetrics and tropical medicine. She married a Swedish school teacher, and continued to live there surrounded by children, grandchildren and a great many friends.

29
Fifth Grade, 1942-1943

In 5th grade we got a new teacher. She was young, probably mid-twenties, smiled a lot, and was energetic and fair. We thought she was wonderful and adored her. This was the year we worked very hard on grammar and sentence structure. We became experts on "analysis", and impressed the district superintendent when he came visiting. We could find and name all the various components of any sentence, all the verb forms, all the declensions, and we even used Latin names.

This knowledge became even more helpful later when we started to learn other languages. In 6th grade we began German studies and in high school we added English and French. Having the excellent background in grammar made those studies less formidable.

We had a poetry reading contest that year. We could pick any poem, memorize it and recite it in front of the class. Then we voted on who the winner would be. The teacher had the final say. It turned out that the two finalists were my best friend Anne Marie and I. We had both picked nature poems, and both were about a winter landscape. Anne Marie's father had composed hers. Mine came from a book. There was some discussion about which poem was best and who recited it best. The majority thought I should win. The teacher agreed. I was so proud and happy, because the prize was a book and in it the teacher wrote: "This book was given to Hanna because she was the best at reciting poetry." That book was one of the few treasures of my childhood. I read it over and over, and showed it to all the people who came to visit us.

I liked reading, and would borrow books from all my friends. I was especially fascinated by the Nancy Drew series. In Norwegian they were called The Miss Detective Books. I read all of them, often walking long distances when I heard that someone had a new book.

We had no school libraries nor public libraries where I lived, so I just read whatever I could find.

In our home we had some books as well, and I read them all, including some with explicit sexual scenes. I was intrigued about those, but knew better than to ask Mama what all of that meant. Most of the books were quite wonderful and taught me a lot. One of them was titled *Thora's Summer Trip to Saga Land.* I read it 13 times. It was about a high school girl who won a trip to Iceland where she visited all the historical places. I learned about the old Icelandic sagas which are stories about individuals and families, strife and battles, but also about adventures, all of which happened a thousand years ago.

Another happening in 5th grade was quite traumatic. We were having a written geography test. We noticed that a girl, who had just joined our class from another community, was cheating. She kept her geography book open under the desk and peeked in it. The teacher saw it too. She became furious. She pulled the book out, closed it and smacked it on Ellinor's desk three times while saying in a loud, high-pitched voice, *"Fy skam! Fy skam! Fy skam!!!"* (Shame on you! Shame on you! Shame on you!!!)

Then she gave us all a lecture on honesty and said that she would never tolerate any cheating in her class room. We were stunned, for we had never seen this teacher angry before, and we felt both sad and ashamed on Ellinor's behalf. She was crying, hiding her face in her arms while her shoulders shook. We continued with our test, but the silence in that room almost made it hard to breathe. As each of us finished, we packed up and went home, for it was the last hour of the school day. Ellinor remained behind. We wondered what would happen to her.

The next day she was happy and smiling, as was the teacher. We asked Ellinor what had happened after we left. "We talked," she said. She would not say any more, and we understood that they had made up with each other. This incident was never mentioned again and none of us was caught cheating, for it was completely foreign to us.

Our teacher would let us borrow books from her own library to take home. I borrowed one about a Norwegian girl who won an Olympic medal in downhill skiing in 1932 or '36. I promised I would take very good care of it.

One day when I was out playing my brother found it, and scribbled on the cover with a brown color pencil. I was devastated. How could I tell the teacher? Would she be as angry with me as she had been with Ellinor? I tried to erase the pencil marks, but could not.

Mama said I had to be brave, tell the teacher exactly what had happened and take the consequences. The book had been my responsibility and I had left it out for my brother to find. She also said that we would offer to pay for the book, although it could not be replaced.

I knew she was right, but oh, how scared I was! I prayed all evening that God would grant a miracle and keep the teacher from being angry with me. And if she was angry that I would react in the right way. I did not quite know what the right way was, but I was sure God did.

I had a terrible stomachache as I walked to school with that despoiled book in my satchel.

As soon as the teacher arrived I went up front with the book and told her everything. She looked at the book, then she looked at me, and she had such a mild, kind look on her face.

"Oh, that does not matter," she said. "Did you read the book?" I answered that I had.

"What did you think of it?" she asked. I told her. She told me I did not have to pay for it, because it was just the cover, not the book itself, that was marked.

When I walked back to my desk I felt so immensely relieved and happy, and I loved my teacher even more. I also closed my eyes and thanked God that the miracle had happened.

Our teacher lived in Narvik, so she had to cross the harbor by ferry every morning. Sometimes we would go down to the ferry dock and meet her, but most of the time we would wait for her in the classroom. One dark winter morning we decided to play a trick on her. We hid under our desks, and turned the light off. I hid in front, under the teacher's big desk which we called *Kateter*. When we heard her in the hallway we were quiet as mice. She opened the door, turned on the light, and said in her friendly, cheerful voice, "I know you are here, so good morning to all of you!" Then she removed her coat and hat and hung them on the peg by the door. She came walking to her desk saying, " Today we are going to…" Just then I stuck my hands out, and crawled up her legs with my fingers. She let out a scream and jumped back. The whole class roared as I crept out. She was a good sport and laughed with us. We thought it was so funny, "Today we are going to... SCREAM."

When I told Mama about this she looked both amused and disapproving. " You are lucky she did not get mad at you. I think you had better not do anything like that again." But all of us in the class had so much fun reliving and retelling that story for several days.

The day before the last school day we stayed behind after the teacher left. It was the end of June. We decorated the room with fresh birch branches and streamers of crepe paper. Then we bought flowers for her, several potted plants, like roses and fuchsias and geraniums, which we placed on the *Kateter*. We thought the room looked beautiful.

The very last school day we did not do much work. We sang, read poetry and wrote an essay, "What I Liked About Fifth Grade." She gave us our grade books. I expected to get all A's, and I did. Then we said goodbye to her, for she was going to get married and would not teach next year. Since she could not carry all her plants and teaching material alone, three of us took the ferry with her, and helped her get everything home.

It was a long walk from the ferry dock to her home, about twenty minutes or so. She lived with her parents in a very nice home. We were invited into the salon, and given raspberry *saft* to drink—very special and delicious. Her father was there, so we talked with him for a few minutes. I wanted to tell him how much we liked her, and what a nice person she was. I said: "You have every reason to be proud of your daughter!" He smiled and thanked me. Then we left.

When we were outside Anne Marie and Greta exploded in laughter. They mimicked me: "You have every reason to be proud of your daughter! Oh, Hanna, you are so dumb! Hahaha! What were you trying to be? An aristocratic lady, putting on airs? Hahaha!"

They laughed and laughed, stopped and lifted their faces up to the sky, and laughed some more. I felt so humiliated. I had just wanted to tell him how I felt. I was so hurt that I did not say anything more the whole way back. When I told Mama about this she said: "Perhaps they were just jealous that they couldn't have thought of it first. What you said was just fine, so don't think about it anymore." I felt comforted. Mama always understood.

Hanna and her fifth grade friends.
Back row: Greta, Hanna, Marit, Synnøve, Anne Marie
Front row: Sussi, Ellinor

30
Christmas Eve

Each year as December arrives, Northern Norway is fully into what is called *Mørketiden,* the dark time. The sun has disappeared, and there is only a short period of daylight. By Christmas at Ankenes it would be light about 11 a.m. and by 1:30 p.m. the darkness was back again. Most days we had the indoor lights on all the time.

Yet Christmas is called *Lysets Høytid,* the solemn festival of light. Outside, darkness has settled over the region, but inside, the houses are filled with light, both the regular electric lights and the *levende lys* (the living lights, or candles). In the window sills and on every table and shelf candles are burning.

One of the Christmas songs says, *"Da tenner moder alle lys så ingen krok er mørk,"* "Then mother kindles all the lights so no corner is dark." In the shopping centers white lights hung across the streets and buildings.

The month of December up to Christmas Eve was spent getting ready. The whole house had to be washed—ceilings, walls, windows and floors. All the lace and cotton curtains were taken down, laundered, starched and ironed. Mama spent long days in the cellar wash room. The special Christmas tablecloths and runners were also made ready.

We children had the job to polish copper pieces and silverware. Mama scrubbed the long, woven floor runners, *Mattene,* on the washboard, section by section. They became very heavy, so it was hard work to rinse and hang them out on the clothesline to freeze-dry.

Before the war a great deal of food preparation went on. Fish and meat were salted, cured and put away in the cellar. Breads of various kinds came, fragrant from the oven, and seven kinds of cookies filled cake tins—*Hjortetakk, Fattigmann, Berlinerkranser, Serinakaker, Goro, Pepperspisser* and *Sandkaker*—which also were stacked away.

New Christmas clothes were generally part of the tradition. Mama sewed most of them. Vesla and I got dresses the same color. Odny and Torgunn got another color, and Marit and Ingebjørg a third. During the winter we wore knitted, brown or gray woolen stockings, but for Christmas Mama knitted or bought white ones.

Christmas was the most wondrous celebration of the year.

By December 23rd, called *Lille Julaften* (Little Christmas Eve), most of the work had been done. The house smelled clean and new. Only the tablecloths and runners had to wait for Christmas Eve to be put in place. On *Lille Julaften* we got to taste the cookies for the first time. It was a special moment when the platter of these cookies, made only once a year, were placed on the table, and we got to help ourselves to one of each kind.

This was also the night of the Christmas bath. Our hair was washed with *Grønnsåpe*. This was a semi-solid green-brown soap, generally used for cleaning the house. Then Marit put our wet hair up in *Papillottes* (French for butterflies, actually curlers). She folded pieces of paper into narrow strips, and wound strands of hair around them. The strip was tied into a knot. Oh, how uncomfortable it was to sleep on those knots, but we were told we had to *"Lide for skjønnheten"* (suffer for beauty's sake).

Christmas Eve morning we would awaken early, and just lie in bed for awhile, talking about the day ahead. Mama still had much to do, so we stayed out of her way, or helped if we could, but the hours were extra long.

Then came 1 p.m. We had our *lutefisk* dinner. *Lutefisk* is dried cod, first soaked in water, then in a lye solution to soften it, then in water to remove the lye. It takes many days to get it ready for cooking. It is traditionally served with boiled potatoes and melted butter, and in my family with *brun gjetost* (brown goat cheese) and *"grønnerte-stuing"* (dried green peas cooked to a mush). Christmas had started.

After the dishes were done, the special tablecloths, runners and candles were put in place. Now it was time to put on our new clothes, get all the *papillottes* out, brush and comb our by now badly tangled hair, and have the big *hårsløyfe*, the taffeta ribbon bow, tied in it. We felt so beautiful, and so ready to receive the special *Julegjest,* the Christmas Guest, which we knew was the unseen Child Jesus. He was the one who would bring the inner joy to us this Christmas season.

At 5 p.m. the Children's Christmas Service started. We put on our heavy winter coats, scarves around our necks, mittens and boots, but the newly curled hair with the big bow had to be left uncovered. Then we walked to church.

Through the darkness shadows moved across the snow-covered road, from both directions to the white, octagonal church on the hill. As they passed under the street lights we could make out who they were. The noise of work had stopped across the harbor at the iron loading docks, and a great stillness had descended over our community. It was called *Julefreden,* the Christmas peace.

On the church steps we stamped our feet to get the snow off before walking quietly into God's Holy house. Here the candles were burning, and the organ played. There were no electric lights on Christmas Eve and the flickering flames made our shadows dance, like magic.

The church was not heated, and all sounds echoed around us. We hardly noticed how cold it was as we sang and sang and sang, all our beloved Christmas hymns—*Jeg er så glad hver julekveld* (I am so happy each Christmas Eve), *Jeg synger julekvad* (I sing the Christmas songs), *Kimer, I klokker* (Ring, ye bells), *Et barn er født i Betlehem* (A child is born in Bethlehem), *Her kommer dine arme små* (Here come your little children), and *Glade jul, hellige jul* (Joyous Christmas, holy Christmas, or Silent Night, Holy Night).

The pastor had a white shawl over his black robe with the white piped collar. He talked to us about the real meaning of Christmas. We sang some more.

When the organ stopped playing there was a moment of utter silence. Then the bells started chiming. Ding dong, ding dong, ding dong!

Fast and joyously they rang, filling our ears and hearts as we hurried home to where the Christmas porridge waited. But first we shook hands with neighbors and friends, wishing them *God Jul,* Good Christmas!

Mama had set the table while we were gone. Our best dishes and gleaming silverware beckoned us on a white shiny cloth.

A basket filled with tulips and hyacinths, cultivated in the greenhouses especially for Christmas, stood on a red runner, with sprigs of evergreen with little red and white artificial mushrooms interspersed between the blooms. The fragrance filled the room.

Mama or Papa read the Christmas story from the Bible. We held hands and sang our table prayer, *"I Jesu navn går vi til bords   Å spise, drikke på ditt ord   Deg Gud til ære oss til gavn   Så får vi mat i Jesu navn."* "In Jesus' name we go to the table   To eat and drink by Your word   To God the honor, ours the gift   So we get our food in Jesus' name." Then we started to eat.

The Christmas porridge, *(risengrøt),* was made of white rice, dotted with brown raisins and had a little well of melted butter in the middle. We sprinkled sugar and cinnamon on, and ate it slowly, savoring each bite. One of us would get the blanched almond in our portion, and receive the special *Mandelgave,* the almond gift. It meant the lucky one would have an extra good year. The gift was usually a marzipan pig, which we shared with the rest of the family.

After the rice porridge which we had only at Christmas, we walked around the Christmas tree, holding hands and singing. We sang the hymns, but also special Christmas play songs, such as: *"Jeg gikk meg over sjø og land, der møtte jeg en gammel mann,"* "I walked over sea and land, there I met an old, old man." As we sang we would do several motions this old man did.

Odny's best friend, Sissel, lived in the house closest to ours, across the field. She was an only child. She told Odny that she would sit by her window and watch us walk around the tree, a big circle of tall and small and middle-sized people passing inside our window. She always wished that she too had a big family on Christmas Eve.

Our *Juletre* (Christmas tree) was a rather short, plump pine bush, which we had decorated with heart-shaped shiny-paper baskets and other decorations we had made in school dur-ing December. It also had live candles, stuck into little metal birds clamped onto the branches. They were lit only while we walked around the tree. Everyone had to watch the candles very carefully to make sure the flames would not touch a branch.

This was the time our Papa was called out for some reason, and while he was gone *Julenissen,* the Norwegian Christmas elf, our Santa Claus, arrived.

We sat down and received our presents, two or three, each. Most of them were clothes which we needed, but we usually got one special gift, such as a book or a table game, or perhaps a ring or a necklace. How very precious that was! There might even be a pair of skis or a sled or a *spark* waiting outside in the dark. When Papa returned we told him all about *Nissen,* and how sad we were that he had missed him. He said he thought he had seen him leaving our house.

After the gifts were opened we sat down at the table again for more special Christmas food. There were breads and cheeses, cured meats, pickled herring, sweet jams, and finally the cookies. Oranges and red apples, dates and figs, bowls of various types of nuts with a nutcracker were placed on the little tables. So many good things to eat! We read or played or talked for awhile, or just sat quietly enjoying the lights and warmth and special smells of Christmas. Finally we were ready for bed after a long day. Another wonderful Christmas Eve was over.

The Occupation markedly changed our Christmas Eve celebration.

We still had lights inside, but none in the window sills. The black shades covered the glass tightly. We could no longer look out and see the neighbor's windows and rooms alight. When we walked outside it was very dark, except for the moon and the Northern lights on cold, clear nights.

No street lights were allowed. Each person had a luminous little tag called *Blendingsmerke* (blackout mark) attached to our coat lapels. The manufacturers became quite creative, and made them in various designs. Now we could tell that people were moving a distance away on the road by these little tags bobbing up and down and sideways.

The Christmas Peace was disturbed by the presence of the loud Occupying forces, their trucks, horse wagons and parades, always some motion on the roads.

Mama still cleaned the house from top to bottom, but soap was hard to come by. She made her own soap using tallow and cod liver oil, pot ashes and caustic soda, which she cooked. When it cooled it turned into hard, light-brown chunks which did not smell good.

We were able to buy rationed "B-soap" for personal use. It felt and looked like a piece of clay, and did not foam or smell, but did a fair job of cleaning dirty hands. It was not good for shampooing.

During the war we did not take new clothes for granted either. The stores were empty. Sometimes Mama would get some old clothes, take them apart at the seams very carefully, clean and press the pieces, and make new outfits. At times several garments were combined, and the resulting creations were often quite interesting.

But the biggest difference for me between pre-war Christmas and those during the Occupation was the food. We had very little sugar, no margarine or butter, no white flour, no eggs, no rice, little milk or other dairy products such as cheese, no raisins or nuts or fruits. Meat was non-existant as well. For our Chistmas porridge we got something called *Hirsegryn* (millet). It was a bit like American corn meal, and foreign to us. We liked it quite well. People made cakes from potatoes, dark flour, oats, barley and whatever was available. We called it *Krisemat*, crisis food. At times we could buy sweetened condensed milk. Mama saved a can or two, and cooked it for several hours in a pot of water. It turned into a caramel-tasting spread. We thought it was delicious.

Except for the last winter, 1944-45, we usually had fish, potatoes, herring, and perhaps root vegetables in the cellar. Though the food was inferior, we still had a beautiful Christmas table.

We had the tree and the candles, the warmth and the songs, the clean, fresh-smelling house, and even a few presents, mostly things made of paper or wood.

And each year we talked about how it used to be before the war, and how it would be again after the war. *"Når krigen er slutt,"* "when the war is over," was our everyday song of hope.

31
The Nazi's Iron Fist

When the German flagship *Blücher* sank in the Oslofjord April 9th, 1940, a large portion of the German police forces, including the secret police, called Gestapo (or *Geheime Staats Polizei*) also perished. But it did not take long before the arrests started. The first were British citizens living in Norway. They were suspected of being agents of the Secret Service. Next came the Norwegians who openly showed their contempt of the occupation forces.

After Terboven arrived he immediately declared the right to use German police to enforce his ordinances. May 16th a new contingent of Gestapo arrived. The arrests increased.

The Oslo prison in Mollergaten 19 normally housed 145 prisoners. By August 1940 it had 550 inmates. The same happened in all prisons throughout Norway.

Then the abuse started. The abuse turned to torture. Brutal kicks and beatings during interrogations were common. Finger- and toe-nails were ripped out, body parts burned with cigarettes, pliers and vises and torture instruments known from the Middle Ages were used. The prisoners were choked and had their joints dislocated.

Such horrors were almost unbelievable and incomprehensible to a nation which was law-abiding, peace-loving and gentle. The death penalty had been abolished in 1902, except for the military penal code in case of treason. The last execution took place in 1848.

On December 12th the Supreme Court judges resigned in protest. They could not accept Terboven's claim to supplant Norwegian Law. In early 1941 after the protest letter by forty-three Norwegian organizations, representing 750 thousand Norwegians was sent to Terboven, he became furious.

Then Himmler arrived. He had been head of Germany's police, including the *Gestapo* since 1936, and had started his career with "the blood purge" of 1934. He was behind the mass murders in the German concentration camps. That same month, June, a new group of the *Gestapo* arrived from Poland.

On July 31st, 1941 Terboven asserted his right to declare martial law or civil emergency, and establish tribunals to try and to convict any person charged with resistance to the occupying forces. Resistance meant "any action that threatens order and security, the economic life and the workplace."

Terboven felt that he had tried to win the Norwegians by reason and persuasion, but when the soft approach did not work he would have to resort to force. The Norwegian laws were declared null and void. *Höherer* SS and *Polizeifuhrer* (higher ranking storm troopers and police leaders) would make all decisions necessary to maintain order and security.

Those convicted would be sentenced to imprisonment for 10 years or up to life, or condemned to death. Death sentences would be carried out immediately by firing squads.

All radio receivers would be confiscated, delivered to the sheriff or police within 5 days, to "protect the population from the lies and poison flowing from the high seat of Jews, goldmongers and capitalists," in other words, from London. NS members were allowed to keep their radios.

This was the last news the Norwegians heard on their radios. From then on any radio receiver found in any home would mean a death penalty for the owners.

A heavy, dark cloud of fear seemed to suffocate the nation.

Up to this time people had been able to listen to BBC (British Broadcasting Corporation) not only in English but also in Norwegian. Both the King and government leaders had spoken to the Norwegian people that way. Now, no encouragement from abroad.

The law-abiding people complied. They had little choice—all radios were registered since there was an annual listener fee. Some who had two radios were able to hide one, and their hiding places were creative and as safe as possible. They knew what it meant if they were discovered. Who had the radios and where they were hidden only very few knew. It was best not to know.

One man kept his radio on his fox farm, in the food preparation building, under some loose floor boards. It was well known that foxes were very temperamental and super-nervous animals. If a fox mother became frightened, she would kill and eat her babies. Only the regular caretakers were allowed near the cages, and big signs were posted all around the farm warning unauthorized persons to keep out. The Germans loved the Norwegian silver fox furs, and wanted them for their sweethearts and wives, so they never interfered with the farm.

And so the news from England leaked out, by word of mouth, but also through the illegal newspapers, bulletins and other underground writings. This was the way we learned how the war really was going in the rest of the world.

On September 6th and 7th, 1941, British planes flew over Oslofjord several times. They dropped some bombs near Oslo and in the harbor. People flocked to the streets, windows and rooftops instead of going to the shelters. They cheered and applauded, especially when one of the planes wrote the V-sign and H-7 with smoke in the sky.

The next day, Monday, September 8th, Norwegians could not get their milk rations, but delivery to the Germans went on unhindered. The same thing happened Tuesday. Work stopped all over Oslo. Over fifty factories went on strike.

On September 10th big posters everywhere declared that martial law was now in effect, and military court martial established. Some of the factories received German guards.

The same day two Norwegians who had been arrested previously, a young lawyer, Viggo Hansteen and a metal worker, Rolf Wickstrom were executed. Their clothes were brought to their families with no explanations.

That was the beginning of the executions.

On September 11th Norway's only university received a letter calling all professors and students to a meeting in the University *Aula* (auditorium) at 5 p.m. The president was fired and later imprisoned. The University's battle is a long and complicated story in itself, but many of the students were very active in the resistance movement and many ended up in German concentration camps.

That same day Oslo radio announced, after first playing funeral music, that more people had been condemned to death or given long prison sentences. The latter meant being sent to Germany, which often meant dying without a formal death sentence.

Officially the civil emergency was called off September 16th, but in reality it continued. German *Sicherheitspolizei* (security police) expanded, and started to map the resistance groups, to break them by *razzia* (raids) and torture. Some of the worst torture took place in September, 1941 and after.

Later on Quisling started a mobilization of Norwegian citizens under the cover name The National Work Service, A-T (*arbeidstjeneste*). The Underground sent out *paroles* (instructions) to the Norwegian police that they should not promote or enforce this.

A Norwegian policeman, Gunnar Eilifsen, refused an order to pick up two girls who had been called to work service. He was brought to court martial and executed.

The iron fist was evident.

Trials were closed to the public. The proceedings were conducted without the various steps of a formal trial. There was no opportunity for adequate defense. The sentence was carried out shortly after being pronounced. During the occupation 366 Norwegians were executed by the Germans. Over a thousand died in concentration camps. Thirty

141

eight died from torture. Forty-eight committed suicide rather than risk divulging secrets.

As the Underground movement grew and became better and better organized, the risks also increased. NS people and double agents managed to infiltrate in spite of all precautions. One of the most infamous was *Rinnanbanden*, the Rinnan gang.

Henry Oliver Rinnan was a scarcely-five-foot-tall man who lived in Trondheim. He entered a pact with the Germans in 1940 to become an informer and *provocateur*. He bragged openly about this. One man asked him, "What would the Germans want with a little shrimp like you?" That remark later cost him his life. Rinnan personally tortured him severely, then killed him.

Under the name of Olaf Whist, Rinnan acted as a British agent, and caused an enormous amount of harm to the Underground. He and his gang of about thirty were responsible for exposing and arresting over a thousand of the resistance participants, of viciously and systematically torturing several hundred, and getting nearly a hundred executed.

Often whole communities were punished when a resistance "nest" was uncovered, or acts of sabotage took place. Homes were burned, their inhabitants sent to prison or concentration camps, and executions followed.

After the British Lofoten raid March 4th, 1941, Terboven himself flew up north and started the act of revenge. He ordered a great many houses burned, and took a large number of hostages, who were sent south to prison camps.

Southwest of Bergen on a small island called Sotra lay a fishing village, Telavåg. It was a resistance center with direct contact with England. In April, 1942, two Norwegian agents just arrived from England were surprised by an SS troop from Bergen. During the arrest one of the agents was killed, but he had already shot two of the German officers.

The punishment was severe. All the seventy-six adult men of the village were sent to German concentration camps. Only thirty-five survived. The rest of the population, 260, were interned in other places in Norway and all the houses were burned to the ground. The other surviving agent was executed of course. But that was not enough. The same hour the two German officers were buried in Bergen, eighteen young men imprisoned at Grini, Oslo for trying to escape to England were executed.

The German reign of terror reached into every part of Norway.

The Norwegians believed the Allies would soon invade and bring delivery from this occupation nightmare. England had sent boatload after boatload of weapons, ammunition and food, which men from the Underground carried on their backs over the mountains to hiding places. Each time a boatload arrived the men were told that the invasion would soon happen, and they should get more people to carry. But the spring of 1942 came and went, and no invasion. In July the last boatload arrived, and again they were assured the invasion was imminent.

The Germans were in trouble on the Russian front, and the resistance movements in all the occupied countries increased. So did the activities of the Gestapo and of the Norwegian traitors.

One of the most horrible incidents was the Majavatn case, where twenty-two men from one resistance group were taken and condemned to death. The youngest was sixteen years old, but his sentence was commuted to life in prison. The evening of October 9th, the radio announced that these men had been executed. The condemned were allowed to hear that announcement. Early the next morning they were taken out into the woods and shot.

In another community a seventeen-year-old youth, Odd Tveit, stood in front of his house and waved to a Russian prisoner walking by on the road. He was arrested. First he was taken to the local prison, then to the regional one. From there his journey led to Grini, and finally to Sachsenhausen, Germany. He died there, eighteen years old. He was his parents' only child.

In spite of vigorous propaganda, NS could never muster more than about 43 thousand members at its peak in 1942, declining from then on. We knew who they were, but we did not always know who "the striped ones" were, the collaborators and informants. And so we spoke carefully. Even children knew that conversations we overheard at home should not be repeated. We had a sense of who the "good" people were, but others we were not so sure of.

The huge posters with new Terboven edicts were read and discussed at home. Terboven became synonymous with "Terror." The newspapers listed the names of those executed. Posters with names inside black borders were pasted to telephone poles. I always got that awful feeling in my stomach when I learned that more men had been shot. They were usually young men.

One man from our region, Ernst Hekkelstrand, was executed November 3rd, 1941, on my brother's birthday, which we had celebrated in our new house. He had tried to flee to England on a fishing boat with six other men. His parents wrote to Terboven, asking him to spare their son. But there was no mercy.

Every execution increased our sense of dread and apprehension. No one was safe. We seemed to be surrounded not only by thousands of *Die Wehrmacht* soldiers, but also all kinds of different *Polizei.*

We had men with SS on their arms. It meant *Schutzstafel* (storm trooper), and then the *Gestapo,* the secret, but very visible, police. Then we had SuSD, *Sicherheitspolizei und Sicherheitsdienst* (security police and security service). SS provided the firing squads.

From September 17, 1942, the *Reichskommisariat* alone was responsible for the civilian sector in Norway, and *Der Fuhrer's* representative there. Quisling was used when it was an advantage to do so, otherwise he was ignored.

Quisling and his government failed to Nazify the schools, control labor, sports and athletics, the Church or the youth. He was supposed to be the head of the National Government, but he had no nation that wanted to be governed by him. The New Order was rejected by the Norwegian people.

But he was still instrumental in bringing great harm and evil to the nation. He had his own *Hird*, his own SS, his own political police, *Stapo* (state police) and *Sipo* (state security), his own "People's Court," his own informers and torturers.

In March, 1945, when they saw which direction the war was heading, one of his own ministers, Finn Storen remarked, "I have a feeling that the German authorities are deliberately making a fool of you, *Herr Ministerpresident,* and of *Nasjonal Samling.* Under a pretense of friendship and cooperation they managed to make our administration share their guilt as plunderers and oppressors."

The iron fist had fallen hard on Norway. The New Order was not a good order. We waited and longed for the day when everything would be back to normal again. Never for a moment did we doubt the arrival of that day. We just had to live as best we could, be patient and wait. But we grieved deeply all those who gave their lives in the fight.

An Underground poet wrote:

> *Vi er så få her i landet*
> *hver fallen er bror og venn.*

> We are so few in this country
> each fallen is brother and friend.

We nodded our heads solemnly when we read that. He had spoken our deep feelings.

32
Traveling South, by Boat

During the occupation people needed official permission documents to travel from one place to another. My sister Marit's fiance had worked in Northern Norway while she was a housekeeper for an older man in Hamar, her fiance's hometown. Now he was returning, and somehow the idea came up that I could go with him.

I was 11 years old, small and skinny for my age. Food was hard to get, and I also had a very strong dislike for some foods that were available, such as cod liver oil, margarine made from herring oil, herring soup, and so forth. Often I was hungry because I just could not eat what the others ate. Fish fried in cod liver oil made me gag.

Hamar, which is in the southern part of Norway, was surrounded by large farms, so food was more plentiful, especially dairy products, which we could hardly get at all up north.

Mother took me to the local physician who wrote a letter to the authorities saying that a stay in the south would be beneficial to my health. So they gave me a travel permit.

Oh, how excited I was! To travel for many days by boat and train! I had never been on a big coastal steamer or on a train. All the things I would see that I had only read about filled me with great joy. I would see the big, medieval cathedral in Trondheim. I would see electric street cars running on tracks, the largest fresh water lake in Norway, apple trees and pear trees. Fruit trees could not grow as far north as Narvik. where we lived. This was the greatest adventure in my whole life. I really liked my sister's fiance. His name was Arvid, and he was like my big brother. I had always wanted an older brother. I had only older sisters. Some of my friends who had big brothers thought they were extra nice, because they could build things, and they always gave special gifts for birthdays and Christmas.

One early summer evening in 1943 we boarded the smaller local ship that would sail all night, with stops in many places. In the morning we would arrive in Svolvær, in the Lofoten islands.

At this time of the year it was light night and day in Northern Norway. I stood on the deck for many hours that night as we sailed out the fjord. What struck me especially was to see how the mountains changed shape as we sailed on. We called most of them by name, and often they had the shape of humans or animals. But now they became all distorted, were shorter or stuck out when seen from another angle. I could hardly recognize them. It felt a little frightening to me. What I had always known to be so solid and big and unchangeable suddenly turned out to be quite different when seen from another side or from the back.

I finally got sleepy. Arvid found a place in the big passenger lounge where I could lie down. I curled up in a corner with my sweater for a pillow, and my coat for a cover. The next morning I felt a bit queasy when I woke up, but going out on deck for some fresh air helped. We ate the waffles and rhubarb jam we had brought along in an empty shoe box, and drank some stale lukewarm water from the carafe in the passenger lounge. There were several lounges, called *salons.*

In Svolvær we were to board the big coastal steamer, the *Hurtigruten* (the express route) in early afternoon for the forty-hour trip to Trondheim. It was delayed for several hours. Fortunately Arvid knew some people in Svolvaer. We stayed there while we waited. They gave us dinner too. Late in the afternoon we heard the horn tooting. The steamer had arrived.

We boarded after we had gone through the controls where our tickets and travel permits were checked. We could not get cabins. They were all taken by Germans and NS people, but again we found a place in one of the salons where we would spend most of the 40 hours of this part of the journey. In spite of a scarcity of tobacco, people smoked everywhere. I got a severe headache and felt nauseous from all that smoke.

One stretch of water we had to cross is an open piece of ocean where the Atlantic comes in unsheltered by islands or reefs. It was called Folla. In winter it could be very stormy and rough. Almost everyone had heard of "feeding the fish over Folla." It meant getting seasick and throwing up.

Now it was summer, the weather was nice, and the ocean calm. Still, the big ship rolled slowly from side to side because of the undertow. I thought it looked very strange through the windows. For a few seconds we saw the gray ocean, then it moved down and away, and we saw only sky and clouds, then back down to the ocean again. Sea and sky, sea and sky. I started to feel more queasy and headachy, so Arvid thought we should go out on the deck. The sea air blowing in my face felt so clean and refreshing. Huge seagulls followed the ship, crying like a cat's high pitched mew, the engines rumbled and made the ship vibrate, and people walked back and forth with their coats buttoned all the way to the chin.

The ship made several stops before we got to Trondheim. Each one seemed similar. The big horn blew, the engines slowed, and the ship eased up to the dock. The young deckhand tossed a thin rope. It whizzed through the air. Someone on the dock caught it and hauled it until the big heavy rope attached to the thin one appeared. It had a loop that the man dropped over a big iron knob on the dock. Then he put the gangplank in place, and many passengers left. Others came aboard. Large winches lifted goods of all kinds off and onto the ship. I enjoyed watching all these activities.

Although the mines had been cleared from the main shipping lanes, occasionally some tore loose from mine-belts in other areas. So there were still some risks at sea.

Sometimes we went ashore if the ship was staying for a couple of hours. In Bodø we had enough time to visit my Tante Emma. But we were sure to be back at the dock in good time to board before the gangplank was removed, the horn blew, and the ship pushed off for the next segment of the journey.

One of the most fascinating aspects of the trip was seeing so many mountains with legends attached to them. I had heard these legends, and now to actually see the mountains was special and exciting. Many of the mountains were involved in one legend. It went like this:

The Troll King of Lofoten, named Vågekallen (the old man from Våge), had a frisky, daredevil son, named Hestmannen (the horseman). Across the water on the mainland lived the Suli-king who had seven beautiful daughters. Once, on a visit to the Troll-woman of Landego, these seven sisters went swimming in the ocean on a late summer evening. They bathed nude, and with them was the very fair and lovely maiden Lekamøy (play maiden).

When Hestmannen spotted them he instantly fell in love with Lekamøy. At midnight he set out after her on his horse, galloping across the water. But the bathing girls saw him, and started running southward as fast as they could. When trolls move they create a big, earthshaking racket. This awakened the King of the Somna mountain who observed the chase. Hestmannen shot an arrow after the fleeing girls. The King of the Somna mountain quickly threw his hat between, and the arrow pierced it. Just then the sun rose, and everyone knows that if the sun shines on a troll it turns into stone. That is exactly what happened to these trolls. They became mountains.

Along this watery highway I was traveling I could see these mountains: Vågekallen, Landego, Hestmannen, the Seven Sisters, Torghatten (Torg's hat) with the hole through it, Lekamøy, and many others.

I don't know if I really believed these stories, but somehow these mountains of such different shapes and different names which had supposedly been trolls a long, long time ago were not just massive stone formations but something magical and wonderful.

As we moved south the dialects became noticeably different. I never tired of listening to how the language changed, both the words and the intonation. The farther south, the more sing-song the sentences, and the thicker the consonants. I was truly going far from home in every way.

33
Trondheim and the Train

The ship moved on, and one morning we sailed into Trondheim fjord. Someone said, "Oh, there is Munkholmen!" This is a small island with an old fortress where prisoners were kept. I heard someone else say that they were political prisoners these days.

Trondheim itself had many big buildings, many ships docked at the piers, much activity and lots of commotion. Everywhere I heard the Trondheim dialect. It was so interesting. In Ankenes we had a few people with this dialect, and they really stood out, but here it was the normal way to speak, and my way was the odd one.

We had many hours to wait for the train, so we put our luggage away at the train station and set out to see the city.

The first thing I wanted to do was to ride the streetcar. Arvid was nice, and we boarded one. I think it had a number. Arvid joked, "Streetcars are like girls, if you miss one, there is another one around the corner." We rode to the center of town. There we found an open air market where we bought some fresh, new carrots. We wiped the soil off as much as possible, and munched on them as we walked around. They tasted so good and new and crisp.

The next thing was the cathedral from the middle ages, *Nidarosdomen* (Nidaros cathedral).

Olav Haraldson, a Viking king, brought Christianity to Norway. He fell in the battle of Stiklestad in 1030 and was buried outside the town of Nidaros. Legends soon started about him, and he was declared a martyr and a saint, *Olav den Hellige* (Olav the holy, or Saint Olav). Pilgrims began to arrive from all over Northern Europe, and the church was built to receive them. There is a well inside the cathedral, supposedly built where a spring of holy water appeared the first winter after Saint Olav was buried there.

The Cathedral had been under repair and restoration for over a hundred years. Another legend says that when Nidarosdomen is finished the end of the world will come.

We walked a few blocks and then we could see it—a great, gray stone giant with tall windows, and two towers way up. I had read about it, and wanted to see all: the old altar piece, the stained glass window, the holy water well. And I wanted to just walk where people had walked so many hundred years ago. To my great disappointment the cathedral was locked, so we could not go inside. We walked the whole length of it outside. It was the biggest church, and probably the biggest building, I had ever seen.

By now we were getting hungry, so we looked for a place to eat. This was also exciting. Our family never ate in cafes or restaurants. Arvid said he knew of a place where we could get a meal that was quite reasonable. We had brought our ration cards with us. After some walking we found the restaurant. We had fish cakes in brown gravy with boiled potatoes, and blueberry soup for dessert. It was wonderful.

I tried not to gawk around like a country bumpkin, but there was so much new to see. When I spoke to Arvid, people around us looked at me and asked where in Nordland I came from. They knew from my dialect that I was from Northern Norway. "And now you have traveled so far from home," they said. Yes indeed I had. I felt very lucky and proud. Still we had more to see.

There is an old wooden bridge, *Den Gamle Bybro* (the old town bridge) over *Nidelven* (the river Nid). Every tourist had to see it. I was now a tourist, which I had never been before.

Finally the time for the train journey arrived. The passenger trains were all packed, but at last we found seats at a table by a window and empty baggage racks above. We felt lucky and relieved.

The train did not leave on time, but just sat and sat at the station. People were rushing by outside, this way and that, carrying suitcases and boxes, baskets and bags. We saw lots of German soldiers as well. One came into our compartment. He sat down and started reading. Arvid could speak some German, so they exchanged a few words. I could not wait for the train to start.

At long last the uniformed railroad man outside closed all the doors, blew his whistle, and the engines started jerking the train forward. It moved very slowly at first, then picked up more and more speed.

I asked Arvid if I could go out in the hallway, because a window was pulled down there, and I wanted to see as much as possible. He said I could, but I must not stick my head out the window. Of course I had to try just a little, and exactly at that moment something flew into my eye. Oh, how it hurt! I tried to rub it out, but it did not work.

In the end I had to ask Arvid for help. He borrowed a wooden match from another passenger, turned my eye lid inside out on the match, and with a piece of clean handkerchief he swiped my eye. On the white cloth was a tiny, black particle. I could not believe that such a small thing could hurt so much.

Arvid said it was probably a piece of coal dust. The engines ran on coal, not electricity. Even after it was out, my eye still hurt, so I kept it shut for a while during the next few hours.

From Trondheim we traveled through farmland, then forests, and slowly up into the mountains called Dovrefjell. The houses changed, from big and painted to small and weather-beaten gray. In the curves we could see the whole, long train, leaning in towards the curve. We chugged through tunnels where everything became black, and the clickety-clack sound of the wheels changed and became really loud.

When we came up on the mountain plateau we could see far, far away, across the wide mountain meadows with heather and hills and ponds to snow-capped, blue and white mountains in the distance.

I thought it was very, very grand, and felt a deep love inside me for this my country, called Norway. I knew many songs and poems that fit this view, so I repeated them softly inside myself.

Late in the evening we were down from the mountains again, and now I saw Norway's biggest lake, called Mjøsa. It was very long and wide. All around were large farms with lots and lots of land. I had never seen such a broad valley before. Everything was on a much larger scale than up north.

We got all our luggage down, put our overcoats on, and got ready to leave, for we would soon be in Hamar, where my sister was, and where Arvid's family lived. My long voyage to the south was over.

But the summer ahead seemed endless, and I was full of excitement and expectations at all the new experiences I would have in the weeks to come.

34

Hamar and Arvid's Family

I slept with my sister on the divan in the dining room, and must have been very tired for suddenly I woke up to the sound of people talking around me. They spoke in the sing-song dialect of the south. I had a nosebleed, the first and only one in my life. I was so embarrassed. What a way to start out in a new place.

Three girls were sitting there waiting for me to wake up. One was Arvid's sister. Her name was Ruth. She was a couple of years older than I but looked a lot older because she had breasts and hips, like a woman. The other two were sisters, about my age. Their names were Harriet and Susie. They wanted to welcome me and hear me talk. They laughed at almost everything I said, not in a making-fun-of-me way, but because they thought I was cute. At least, that is what they said. Norway has innumerable dialects, almost one for every little community. Some of them are hard to understand for those who did not grow up in that particular place. In those days a stigma was often attached to particular dialects, and that was the case with the one I spoke. Young people who went south to work tried to hide their accent, and take up the southern way of speaking. But I did not try to do that.

I was eager to go out in the garden and see the apple trees. They thought it was strange that I had never seen an apple tree, and they showed me the pear and plum trees also. It was too early for the fruit to be ripe, but I held the little green balls in my hands being careful not to disturb them. Now I would have more wonders to tell when I went back home.

My sister was the housekeeper for a retired man named Sønsthagen. She had to dust the inside every day in addition to all her other chores. This also was strange to me. In my home we did not dust. Mother washed the tables and counters, the window sills and floors with soap and water. Now I was given a duster, and I dusted all the shelves and tables and the piano every day. I had to move all the photos and figures and vases off first, and then put them back again. I told my sister that I thought it was dumb to dust every day, but she said that was part of her duties. So that became my job while I was there.

We also went shopping for dinner and milk every day. People did not have refrigerators in those days, so the food needed to be bought fresh. I thought it was so wonderful that we could get milk every day, even different kinds of milk: whole milk and skim milk and *kefir* milk which was like buttermilk. It came in bottles with different colored lids for each kind. At home we carried the milk bucket to the store, and hoped we could get our ration of just plain milk that day.

There was also a bakery with good bread, and even pastries. At home the flour was not good, and mother had a hard time making bread loaves that could be cut in slices. Here the flour was not mixed up with fillers which ruined the quality of the baked goods. And in Hamar they could buy fresh, early vegetables. They certainly ate much better in the south than in the north. Arvid's mother was nice to me. She gave me extra goodies—"to fatten you up," she said. I ate cheese and butter, and jams made of raspberries and strawberries and plums. It was almost like being in heaven.

The house they lived in was for four families. It was at the end of a quiet street. Arvid's family lived in one end downstairs, Mr. Sønsthagen lived in the other end. Upstairs were two other families. Facing the street was a big garden with grass and fruit trees, and in the back where all the entrance doors were, stood a woodshed,where they kept a sheep, and an outhouse. There was a court yard as well.

I remember only sunny days that summer. On Sundays and Wednesday afternoons when my sister was off work we sometimes took the bus out to Lake Mjøsa. There on a peninsula stood the ruins of an old cathedral. There was also a beautiful bathing area. I loved going there. The water was so much warmer than in Northern Norway, and although I could not swim I could splash and jump and walk in the water, moving my arms and pretending to swim. In a little white kiosk with a striped awning they sold *ispinner*, (ice pins, that is, frozen fruit bars on a stick). Oh, I just loved those! I was extremely happy when we packed our bags to go there for the day or half day.

Arvid found work in a store. He sold sports equipment and bicycles, suitcases and silverware. The store was owned by a rich farmer. Arvid must have told them that I was there, for they invited us out so I could see a really *big* farm.

One Sunday we went there. The buildings were huge. They had two hundred cows, and the barn where they were kept during the very cold winter was immense. In Northern Norway a big dairy farm might have fourteen to twenty cows. This farm had many outbuildings, including the unique and traditional *stabbur* which is a food storage place. They also had lots of machinery, big, colorful monsters with sharp knives and teeth everywhere. They scared me a bit.

But to top it all, the family lived in two houses, one in the summer and one in the winter. The summer house was smaller, and seemed lower and older to me. The winter house was a grand, white building, which was being cleaned and painted at this time. I had never met such rich people—and I was in awe.

We sat outside, at a little table with white table cloth and pretty dishes. We were served cold waffles with jam, and cool milk to drink. It tasted wonderfully good.

One day Arvid's mother bicycled out into the country where they had relatives. She came home with lots of food. There were big boxes of dark-red cherries. We could eat as many as we wanted. I had never experienced anything like this and could hardly believe it. I ate 123 cherries. I knew because we counted all the cherry pits left on my plate. Afterwards I got a stomachache and diarrhea. That was all right, because usually I was constipated. But all that summer my stomach gave me absolutely no trouble. It was the best summer in all my life.

35
Oslo and the Aunts

Oslo is the capital of Norway. As far back as I could remember that name was magical and shining, for in Oslo the Royal Family lived, including two princesses named Ragnhild and Astrid, and the little prince Harald. The girls were about my age, and to me their lives were not real lives, but an existence far above that of ordinary people. They had everything I did not have, dolls and play equipment, a big doll house with kitchen and living room and furniture they could use and sit on. They had lots of beautiful clothes, winter cabins and summer houses, sailboats and cars and horses. Special books were made about them with lots and lots of photos, and they were also featured in the weekly magazines from time to time.

Now with the war, they had to flee from it all. We heard rumors that they were in America, living with President Roosevelt. If so, I wondered, if they had met Shirley Temple, the world's most beautiful and clever and famous girl film star.

Although the Royal Family had fled, the Royal Palace was still there, as well as all the government buildings, the University, the ski jump Holmenkollen, and the big nature park or wilderness called Nordmarka. I had read about all of this, and formed my own ideas of what all was like.

Now I was actually going there with my sister Marit. Oh, how my stomach tickled as I looked forward to the trip. The train ride would last only a couple of hours, but even that was very wonderful.

We had two aunts in Oslo and one grand-aunt. At Christmas time we got letters from them, sometimes with pictures, so I sort of knew what they looked like. But when we arrived at the train station, I was very eager to see the palace, and so we walked there on a long, straight street called Carl Johan. As we walked along we passed many important buildings. First there was the Grand Hotel where all the famous authors and artists used to eat in the olden days. Then came the University and government buildings, and the Student Park with its huge, old chestnut trees. They were famous too. And at the very end of the street, up on the hill ahead I saw it, with my very own eyes—the Palace! It was a big house with rows and rows of windows, columns in front, the second story balcony where the Royal Family always stood on the 17th of May during peacetime. Oh yes, it looked just like the pictures, but now Quisling had his offices there, while soldiers guarding it marched back and forth in front. We did not get too close but I could tell all my friends at home that I had really been there and seen all these places myself. This was important to me.

We went to visit Tante Anna, Papa's youngest sister. Her husband, Onkel Olav, was a baker. They had a daughter named Gerd-Inger. I don't remember how long we stayed, but we slept on the divan in the living room. Tante Anna curled my long, blond hair with a curling iron she heated on the stove. It was the first time I had my hair curled like that. Then she lent me one of Gerd's hats, and we went to get pictures taken. I still have that tiny picture.

Hanna and Gerd-Inger with curled hair and hats.

Gerd and I rode the street car. We took one called Sagene Ring, and it went around and around the same route. I thought it was wonderful, especially when the bells rang. We also went to a park made especially for children. It had teeter-totters, merry-go-rounds and swings of all kinds. I had never been in a park like that. Gerd thought that was strange. She told all the other children that I came from far up north in Norway, and had never been to Oslo before, had never been to a park like this, and that I just wanted to ride the street car all the time. The children looked at me with wondering eyes.

I believed they thought I was not quite normal, and I felt embarrassed. I wished she had not said anything, but I did not tell her that, or how much it bothered me. Instead I said I wanted to go back to my aunt's apartment.

The toilet was between two floors in the common hallway next to the stairs. It was used by four families, and we needed a huge key in order to get in. Tante Anna's apartment had a dark entry hall, a kitchen, a long living room with lots of furniture, and a bedroom. She had lived there for many years. Late in life, as a widow and alone, she moved into a more modern apartment with its own bathroom.

I liked Tante Anna very much. She played the guitar and sang, she joked and laughed a lot, and had the same eyes Papa did, with the same teasing look.

Tante Tina was my Papa's aunt, his mother's sister. She was a nurse, and still worked at a hospital. She seemed very old to me. She lived in a small house which belonged to the hospital, and was one in a group of houses all the same size. She had only one big room, and a kitchen and entry hall. But on the walls were pictures of her sister— my grandmother whom I had never seen. She died long before I was born. I was named after her.

They had told me that she had been terribly in love with my grandfather, but her parents did not want her to marry him. He did not have a good reputation because he played the fiddle at dances and liked to drink and fool around with the girls. But she had said, "If I don't get him I'll die. If you keep me from marrying him, I will walk out into the ocean and drown myself."

Well, they married, but he turned out to be what her parents had feared. He made good money, but spent it foolishly. The family suffered a great deal from neglect and utmost poverty. Once in a while my dad would tell incidents from his childhood, and we always cried, so he did not want to tell too much.

Tante Tina's neighborhood was beautiful. It was full of trees. I walked around, just looking at all the fine homes with their secluded gardens with lawns, flowers, walkways and outdoor furniture. It was just like a song I knew, a song about paradise. I decided that when I grew up I too would have a house with a fence, a garden with trees and lawn, lots of flowers and walkways, and furniture where I could sit and have something good to eat and drink. It would really be like paradise.

My father's other sister was Constance. We called her Tante Conny. She was married to an engineer. In our eyes he was a special person because his brother Kristian had composed a song that was well-known in Norway, called *"Blåklokker,"* or bluebells. Since his brother was famous we felt the fame rubbed off on Onkel Wilhelm too.

They lived in a suburb of Oslo called Bryn. We took the train out there. Their house was a villa, sort of modern, I think. I remember a big expanse of glass windows, and a wall between the living and dining room which was very unusual, because it did not go all the way to the ceiling. Their home was on a pleasant street with other lovely homes and gardens.

The day we arrived was Onkel Wilhelm's birthday, and they had guests. Tante Conny was very kind to me. It was the first time I met her. She too had eyes like Papa, so I felt I knew her right away. But I did not feel comfortable with my uncle. He made fun of my dialect.

They knew I could recite poetry, and Onkel Wilhelm challenged me to do so. I could not think of any by heart right then, so he gave me a big book with lots of poems which I had not seen before. I did my best, performing for all the guests. When I was done he started to criticize my reading. He was quite unpleasant and I felt hurt. Tante Conny took me out into the kitchen and said I had read very beautifully, and to pay no attention to what he said.

They had two girls and a boy, all much younger than I. In the summer of 1945 they all came north to visit us. At that time I took my cousins up in the hills and all around to show them different places. When they were with us, one of the girls would not drink milk that came from a bucket, so Mama washed some old glass bottles and filled them with milk. Then she drank it. I thought that was strange.

Tante Conny died young from abdominal cancer. Tante Anna told me later that Onkel Wilhelm was a sour and difficult man, and that Tante Conny's life probably was not too happy, although they were financially quite well off. I did not know or understand all of this when I was just 11 years old, but I was very happy to have been able to visit my aunts in Oslo.

There were things about Oslo that were not nice. I knew of course that Quisling lived there. Terboven had taken Skaugum which was the home of the Crown Prince's family. We heard that he had cut down trees there and ruined the place. We had heard of Mollergaten 19, the Oslo prison, and Victoria Terrasse, the *Gestapo* headquarters. People were tortured there. I had no desire to see those places. And outside Oslo was Grini, a very big prison camp with people from all over Norway, some very famous persons among them.

I also saw more *Hird* in their black uniforms than I had ever seen, and of course lots of Germans. But I tried to ignore all of that. To me Oslo was still the city of the King, the city of Government and University, and everything that was great and famous, and I had now been there.

36
Sixth Grade and the Children's Choir

The school year in Norway started the first week of September, so in late August it was time to return home. I felt sad to leave Hamar where I had been so happy.

My sister Marit traveled with me, the same way north as I had come south. First we took the train to Trondheim where we spent a day or two in the home of a girl Marit had gone to school with. They had a musical instrument called a zither. It fascinated me. Soon I figured out how the chords related to each other, and I spent hours playing and singing by myself. How I wished we had one of those!

From Trondheim we again took the coastal steamer to Svolvaer, and then the local ship to Narvik. It had been warm and summery when we left Hamar. At home the leaves were already yellow, the mountain ash berries had turned orange-red, and the mountains were brushed with a thin veil of snow quite far down the sides. In the mornings thin ice covered the water puddles. Fall had arrived up north.

Our sixth-grade class was moved to yet another home, and we had a man teacher. He did not smile very often, but became irritable and loud if things did not go his way. We started learning to calculate with fractions and decimals, converting from one to the other. It was interesting, and also weird that in multiplying one fraction with another the result was less. With whole numbers the result was always more. I could not see why we would ever want to multiply one-fourth by one-fourth. It did not seem to have any practical application. But I dared not tell this teacher so. I just did my work, and did it well.

Not only did we have a change of teachers. The girls I had known so long were changing too. Some of them started to get real breasts. I was still at the nubbin stage, and envied them greatly. In the bathroom we compared sizes, and also how much pubic hair we had. But of course I had been to southern Norway and they had not, so that made up for my other deficiencies.

Something wonderful happened that winter. My sister Marit bought a piano, and left it in our home. She was going to get married in a year, but worked in another town and had no space for it in the little room she rented. My little sister Kirsten and I went from one piano teacher to another, asking if they would teach us, but all had full schedules. At last we heard of a woman who used to teach but no longer did so. We walked to her, up a long hill, and she said yes, she might do it. We were jubilant.

We brought home our first piano books and started practicing. The teacher had said we could try the first three pages. We did six. She sat next to us and just smiled. The next time we also did much more than our assignments. Soon we could play little pieces that sounded like real music. After that came hymns. Our goal was to play Beethoven's *Fur Elise*. We knew a boy who could play it, and we thought that would be the ultimate accomplishment.

I practiced and practiced. One day I was able to borrow a song sheet from a grown up friend. It was a Swedish song about a *Same* (Laplander) girl who lived peacefully among the mountains in Northern Sweden. She longed for the big world outside her home, and one day she left. She spent many years pursuing what she thought were the important pleasures of life, but found little satisfaction in them. Always in the back of her mind was the thought that if only she could return to her childhood home she would be happy again, walking in the mountains, singing songs of gladness and joy.

I learned to play and sing that song by heart, because my friend wanted her music back, and soon I performed it whenever I could. People seemed to like it so much.

My friend Anne Marie and I often went out in the evenings to visit friends or neighbors. One of them was a young man who was recovering from tuberculosis. I think she liked him a lot. Another person we visited was a young widower who had a pump organ. His name was Åge Sletbakk. I asked if I could try the organ. Then I played and sang the *Same* girl song. When I was done he came and sat next to me on the organ bench. He told me that I had a musical gift and ought to develop it. He himself had taken voice training at the Oslo Conservatory and sang solos in churches and at concerts of various kinds. Now he would like to give me voice lessons for nothing.

I was so happy I could hardly breathe. I enjoyed singing and playing more than anything I knew. He taught me how to vocalize, and I sang many beautiful songs at community functions.

One day he decided to start a children's choir. It was a four-voiced choir—first and second soprano, first and second alto. We practiced every Tuesday and Thursday evening. On those nights sixty to seventy children walked along the one road, some from far east, others from far west to an office building in the center of Ankenes where there was an organ. Each section learned their separate voice melody. We learned the words by heart at home. What a wondrous joy it was when we could put all the voices together. It sounded like angels singing. We sang in the two official Norwegian languages (*Nynorsk*, new Norwegian, based on rural Norwegian dialects, and *Bokmål*, formerly called *Riksmål*, which is based on Danish, and spoken in Southeast Norway, especially in the cities), in Swedish and in Latin. We sang serious songs and funny songs and beautiful nature songs.

The *Ankenes Barnekor* got quite a reputation, and we gave concerts in many places, in meeting halls and churches. We also sang at the funerals of two of the choir members who died in a hepatitis epidemic. Those were the saddest times. Our conductor wrote a special song about us with which we opened our concerts. He also changed a patriotic song a bit to give the message that Norway soon would experience springtime after the dark winter was over. Everyone understood the real meaning, that the occupation would end and we would be free again. Whenever it was possible we draped large Norwegian flags on the stage. This was illegal, and could have got our conductor in great trouble, but nothing happened. It was exciting to be daring for our country.

Since I was one of the three soloists I always got terribly nervous before each performance, but when my turn came to sing I somehow forgot there was an audience. My eyes were fixed on the conductor, my voice teacher, and I tried to sing as clearly and well as I could.

On a recent trip to Norway I met with some of the members of that children's choir. More than 50 years later we sat there and sang song after song, and we remembered all the words, even the Latin ones which we did not understand at all. That impressed us. We laughed and cried together thinking back to those days so far away.

I have always been so grateful to this man for the gift he gave us all: two evenings a week for several years, his interest and instruction, his discipline and demand for our best, his wink and smile when we had done a number well, and all the songs we learned. And he got no pay from anyone. He was one of my childhood heroes.

By the end of my 6th grade, the summer of 1944 we were really tired of the occupation. The stores were almost empty, and it was a struggle just to find enough food to survive from day to day. We heard that the Germans were losing the war on every front, and we were even more afraid of what desperate people might do. But we just had to keep going, and hope that soon, very soon, life would be better.

Ankenes Barnekor Note the Norwegian flags on each side and in back. Hanna's face is peeking between the fourth & fifth girl in the front row.

37
The Germans In Our House

In the town of Narvik, and on our side of the harbor, were many German soldiers. They had built barracks everywhere it seemed, and on the roads we could constantly see their trucks and huge horse-drawn wagons. Submarines and other war ships also frequently came into the harbor. Hitler's yacht, *Grille*, was anchored on our side of the harbor for a long time. We heard rumors that German prostitutes were kept there. The yacht was heavily guarded.

The soldiers marched and sang every day, or so it seemed. The Norwegian preschool children would follow behind, marching and singing with them. My brother Knut was one of them. We thought he was cute. *"Heilie, Heilo"* they sang, or at least that is how it sounded to us. Knut had had polio when we were in Harstad, and although his recovery was good, he limped a little to the left side, so we could pick him out among the other children marching.

We children often asked the soldiers for candy, and most of the time they gave us some, or even an apple. They tried to speak in Norwegian, and we laughed our heads off at the way they said our words.

At the very end of the fjord was a Russian prison camp. These prisoners worked on the roads. They looked ragged and hungry, with big dark eyes and very slow movements. When we children passed them, and the German guard was a little way off, they would whisper to us, *"Brot."* We knew it meant bread in German.

Often we would ask Mama for any kind of food and if she had anything, we would furtively give it to them when the guard was not looking. Some guards were nicer than others. Some let the Russians give us things they had made. They carved beautiful peacocks with spreading feathers, all in one piece, or birds pecking at a round dish, or alligators with movable joints. Some were painted, others were not. They were really very pretty. They also made little brass rings. We could trade food for these things if the guards would let us.

School children got dried soup from Sweden which our mothers prepared at home and brought to school to be served at lunch time. This was during the last two years of the occupation. Once we had our German teacher go and ask the guard if we could give our soup to the Russians instead. He shrugged his shoulder, and said OK. Each child in my class brought his bowl to one Russian prisoner. They ate it so fast, and shook our hands to thank us. *"Spasiba,"* they said. We were very happy that day.

Other guards were hard and cruel. I watched them poke the prisoners with bayonets if they did not move fast enough, and shout angrily at them. I wanted to cry every time. We knew that there was a graveyard next to the prison camp and lots of prisoners died in that camp. But it was a forbidden area for us to enter.

One summer day a neighbor stopped by our house. "Last night there was a massacre in the Serbian camp. The guns kept going for hours, far into the night," he said.

Mama sank down on a kitchen chair. "Lord God, what is this evil that has come upon us? Do you mean to say that they just *killed* all these poor, defenseless people?" The neighbor nodded. "They just mowed them down like weeds, hundreds of them." Mama was stirred up. "One day they will pay for it. 'Vengeance is mine,' says the Lord. One day those monsters will meet their Maker. I have to believe that." I felt shaken. I was gripped by feelings of fear and disgust. How could they be so cruel?

But not all were like that. Some Germans were nice. My sister Kirsten even went into the barracks where the soldiers gave her and her friend Solfrid sandwiches to eat. Mama did not want Kirsten to do that.

In sixth grade we started formal German studies. We also had to give up rooms in our homes for the soldiers. We learned to know their names: Hans and Günther and Karl and Fritz and Heinrich. They were not too different from Norwegian names. A couple of girls in my class who went through puberty early started to tease each other about German boy friends, *lieblings,* and they would argue about which of them was the best looking. We began to see the soldiers more as persons from another land than just as "the Germans."

The last year of the war all our bedrooms upstairs and the formal parlor downstairs were taken by the soldiers. First we had an officer with his *Aufpasser,* his orderly, living there. They made one room into a darkroom where they did photo development. We were not allowed upstairs, for anyone caught spying in their rooms could be arrested and possibly shot.

After the officer moved, we got four ordinary soldiers. They were horse handlers. Two of them were friendly. One was from Czechoslovakia. We called him Shablashan, which was as close as we could come to pronouncing his real name. He would often come down in the kitchen with some food for us such as canned meat, a bit of sausage, a piece of cheese, two apples, some dark bread, and so forth. Mama did not know if she ought to take it, but for us there was always a shortage of food, and she was also afraid to refuse it in case it should be seen as resistance to *Die Wehrmacht,* the protectors, as they called themselves. Anything that could be interpreted as resistance was potentially very dangerous.

During most of the war time my older sisters worked away from home. But Odny lived at home for a while, and worked in Narvik. She was considered very pretty. One evening a German soldier knocked on our door. He brought a glass jar of goat milk and sat down. Then he started talking to Odny. He said she was a pretty girl, and he wanted her to go out with him. This was tricky. She could not say yes, and she could not say no. Many Norwegian girls fell in love with German soldiers, and some even had babies with them. The Norwegian people really despised them for associating with the enemy. We didn't think he would force her to go out with him, but we could not be sure.

Fortunately Papa was home just then, so he told the soldier Odny was too young to go out alone with men. This soldier came back often and soon we recognized his footsteps in the hallway, so my sister would quickly hide in another room. Then we would lie and say that she was not home. In this case lying was not wrong, we thought. After a while he stopped coming.

Having a piano was unusual in our community. One evening again there was a knock at our door. A German officer came in and asked if we had *ein Klavier*, a piano. Mama said that we were storing one for our daughter who was away in another town.

We were afraid the officer with the important-looking cap would take it, for the Germans could take anything they wanted or needed. It was called requisition, a new and fancy word. But he asked if he could come and play it. Well, we could only say yes, of course.

We lived in the kitchen, but the piano was in the dining/family room which we did not heat all the time. He started to play, first scales and arpeggios, all kinds of runs up and down the keys. Then he played what sounded like folk tunes, very pretty, and finally some hymns, except they were much more fancy than we were used to. We really enjoyed this, so we kept very quiet in the kitchen. After a while he quit and came out. He clicked his heels together, saluted Mama, and left. We breathed a sigh of relief that he did not take the piano.

He came back many times. Pretty soon we left the door open, and gradually we moved into the room where he was playing so we could watch him as well as listen. One day he took out his wallet and showed us pictures of his wife and two children. They lived in Leipzig. He was worried about them, for Germany was being devastated by Allied bombers, and he had not heard from his family for a long time. He was a member of the Leipzig Symphony Orchestra. The violin was his instrument and he did not play the piano very well, he said. I thought he played wonderfully, but then I was just a beginner. He invited me to play any melody on the treble keys, then he would supply the bass. We had lots of fun doing this.

Suddenly he stopped coming. Many months passed. The war was coming to a close and the Germans were moving south in droves. One day I was standing by the gate to our house. I saw one of the trucks full of soldiers on the road below.

Then one of them shouted, "Hanna, Hanna!" I looked more closely and saw one of them waving his arms to get my attention. He said something more, but I could not catch it. Then he waved one arm in farewell. I was sure it was our Leipzig musician. I hoped he would find his family again. A great sadness spread inside me as I walked up to the house.

38

The Dark Before the Dawn

Papa was away most of the time during my sixth and seventh school year. His company was building a new ferry at a shipyard further south, and he had the responsibility to oversee the engine room installation. I wrote to him regularly and showed off my growing knowledge of German. He in turn would show the letters to the German soldiers who guarded the work setting. He told me they were impressed at how well we could write. I really liked to make my parents proud of me.

One night the Norwegian Underground was able to place explosives on the ferry and it blew up. Papa and two other men were sleeping on board. The ferry was severely damaged, but fortunately the men came away with only minor injuries which was a miracle. Papa's pocket watch was smashed flat from the force of the explosion. Papa and the two other men were arrested.

Rumors were flying that they would be shot for sabotage. One of our neighbors, who was a little strange, came to tell Mama it was certain he would be shot. We prayed and prayed that God would keep this from happening. Mama got a phone call from Papa who said he had been in for interrogation, but he thought the authorities would be sensible enough to understand that they would not have stayed on board and risked their lives if they were going to blow up the ferry. He was right. They were released from prison and he came home for a while.

His nerves were shattered and he was afraid to be alone. This was so strange. My Papa, a grown man, was so afraid that one of us had to stay at home whenever Mama had to leave for a while. He was angry with the Underground, because he said the ferry would not have been finished before the war ended. They, the people who worked on it, would see to that. There would always be some parts unavailable, or something that did not work. He thought that the whole Underground venture in this case was totally unnecessary, and could have been fatal to them in more than one way. After a while he was able to go back south to the shipyard again.

In the meantime the war was going badly for the Germans in Europe and North Africa. Soon we learned they had started to pull out of North Finland and the northernmost part of Norway, because the Russians were coming that way.

As they moved southward they ordered the civilian population to move also, and burned everything behind them. This was called a "Scorched Earth Policy." We did not know how soon it would be our turn.

Marit was married now, and was expecting a baby. She and Arvid decided to go south to Hamar again. Kirsten would go with them. They left in the fall of 1944. The last winter of the war only Mama, Knut and I were left at home. The Germans occupied our whole house except the kitchen and the room next to it. Hunger was always with us.

The farmers and their close relatives in the cities and densely populated areas suffered the least from hunger and malnutrition. Although the occupation forces requisitioned what they needed, and their needs came first, most farmers were able to provide for their families. They had milk and butter, cheese and eggs. They had space to grow produce, especially potatoes and root vegetables. Many had big storage sheds where sacks of various kinds of grains, sugar, coffee and preserved meats were traditionally kept. Right at the start of the war many hoarded as much as they could possibly pay for, and in this way they were spared much of the suffering city people endured.

It did not take long for the warehouses to empty, as the normal peace time trade to the west was cut off. Rationing started in 1940. First were the import foods, such as grains, flour, sugar, coffee, cocoa, syrup and fat. Next year came meat and meat products, eggs, milk and dairy products. In 1942 potatoes and all kinds of vegetables required ration cards.

Unfortunately, it did not help to have cards if the food was not available. Narvik was especially hard hit. Many German soldiers were stationed there, because the city and surroundings were heavily fortified and guarded. The city was also cut off geographically from the farm areas by long fjords which needed ferries for crossing. The road network was poorly developed. The long and rugged coastline, made more dangerous by mines, torpedoes and other war actions, together with an acute lack of freighters to bring goods from the south, made Narvik a real step-child when it came to getting provisions for its civilian population.

Of course we had the railroad to Sweden, but that border was closed as far as we were concerned.

Each fall my parents scrambled to get enough potatoes home for the next year. It was common to figure 100 kilos (220 pounds) per family member per year. If we were lucky we would get carrots and rutabagas too. In September all the school children had to take a week or more off to dig potatoes on the farms. Then we were allowed to buy some for our family.

I enjoyed the potato digging, but it was hard on the back and arms. We were given a hoe with a pointed blade at the end. Then we were assigned a row of potato plants. We would pull the plant up first. On the bottom of it was the "potato mother," that is, the original seed potato. It was all rotten by now. Clinging to the roots were small, white potatoes. In front of us we had two buckets or boxes, one on each side of the row.

Next we took the hoe and dug in from the side, very carefully so we did not cut into the potatoes down in the ground. The idea was to make the first dig deep down, under the roots and lift the potatoes up. And here they came, several of them, yellow-white balls with dirt attached. The tiny and small ones were tossed into one container, the middle and large ones into the other. Some of the "mothers" had many children, others just a few.

Slowly we moved forward, lifting, shaking, digging, plucking and tossing. We needed to be sure we got every single potato in our row.

The September air was crisp, although at times it rained miserably too. Then the fields became a thick mucky brown porridge. But the earth smelled good, and we knew we were doing something important for our family. At night we had rosy cheeks at the supper table. Boiled fresh-picked potatoes with salt and maybe a little margarine tasted so very good.

As the war and occupation dragged on, we were allowed to buy less and less. The flour became almost impossible to make bread from. No matter how long Mama baked the loaves they remained sticky dough inside hard, hard crusts. But we were hungry and we ate it. We would scoop up some of that gummy stuff with three or four fingers, smear some jam or *kaviar* (cod-roe paste) or condensed milk on, and put it in our mouths.

We got very little milk, and when we did it was a feast day. Many, many times I would go out where the milk was kept cool. I would lift the lid and smell the milk, but I could not taste it, for it had to go to our brother. Most days children under six could get their ration.

Margarine was another hard-to-get item. One day we learned that a ship had arrived in Narvik with margarine. Mama said, "Hanna, you are so light on your feet, why don't you take the ferry over and see if you can get some?" We had been without margarine for seven weeks then. I got the ration cards, money and shopping bag and ran off to catch the ferry.

Over on the Narvik side I went to the first grocery store up town. No, they were sold out. On to the next. They still had some, but I was far back in the line, and by the time it was my turn the margarine was gone. I did not have much hope as I came to the third store. I was right, no margarine. My heart was really heavy. I knew Mama would be so disappointed. I prayed: "Dear God, if there is any margarine left please help me find it."

Way down at the other end of town was a little one-man grocery store. In desperation I dragged myself down there. When I asked about margarine, he started to shake his head. Then he looked at me funny and said, "Let me go in the back room and see." He came out with a half-kilo, a beautiful real cube of margarine. Of course I had enough coupons for six kilos, but oh, how glad I was to be able to bring home this precious margarine. The man also gave me a tiny, cone shaped bag with sugar, perhaps a cup full. And to top it off he had some oatmeal too. I paid him and thanked him so very much.

My feet felt light as I hurried up the hill, across town and down the long, sloping street to the ferry dock. "Thank you, dear God, for helping me find the margarine, and for giving me that extra bounty too." It was a happy day.

Many people kept a sheep or a pig or rabbits or chickens in the backyard. Our lot was so full of huge rocks that we could not have any animals or grow anything. It was not possible to rent equipment or machinery, and we could not level it out with our bare hands. We had no relatives with farms either, so we had to do with what we could buy in the stores.

Every day one of us would go to the grocery store to see what had come in that day. Most of the time we could get fish of some sort. On good days we might get some onions or a head of cabbage. Fresh herring was a special find, and if we could buy an egg or two we had hit the jackpot.

I don't know how Mama fed us, but somehow we ate something every day. Once Anne Marie gave me a dead rooster. I carried it home by its legs, but I could not stand to watch Mama pluck it. When it was all prepared I tasted one little bite, but all I could think of was that rooster head with the glassy eyes swinging back and forth on the way home. We were not used to eating poultry anyway.

Now we had very little food. The stores were empty. We had been unable to buy enough potatoes in the fall to last the whole winter as we usually did. The bins in the cellar were almost empty. The bread which Mama baked was hardly edible because seaweed and sawdust were added to the flour. Once in a while we were able to buy our milk ration, but we never saw butter or margarine or cheese, and certainly not any fruits or vegetables.

We did have a barrel of salted herring in the cellar, and Marit sent us five kilogram bags of oatmeal from Hamar a couple of times. That is what we ate three times a day, oatmeal soup and salted herring. I began to have trouble just walking down stairs. I needed to look at each step instead of just running down the way I used to.

The winter wore on. My clothes were threadbare, and my feet often cold, because we could not get anything new. Mama ripped up the seams of one of Papa's old wool shirts. This became a new dress. It even had a velvet collar. She made shoes by layering scraps of fabric onto old socks. They were wonderful in frosty weather, but not so great when it thawed. In the shoe store we could get shoes with wooden bottoms and fish skin uppers, but they did not hold up in the rain.

We heard rumors that Allied forces were marching toward Germany from the West, and the Russians from the east. We heard of severe bombings, that Germany was being completely destroyed. The German soldiers were getting to be both older and younger than they had been at the start of the war. Some said that all those in their 20's were killed.

We had an officer living upstairs for a while. His orderly was only 15 years old. Mama cried. She said, "Lord God, he is just a child. Is he also going out there to be slaughtered? He too has a mother back in Germany I'm sure. She must be so worried about her boy. How terrible war is!"

In April we were told that the end was very near, just a matter of days. There were so many rumors. We did not know what to believe.

The soldiers upstairs started to get drunk and rowdy. They had been very well disciplined up to now. We could hear them arguing loudly. Mama was afraid they would start shooting.

The month of May arrived. Spring was early this year. We could see the sap coloring the birch trees lavender, and the dandelions and yellow buttercups were springing up.

We put on mittens, and went out to gather burning nettles, because we had heard they were edible. Mama cooked them like a stew. They were tough and bitter, but we ate them.

One day we heard that Hitler was dead—Hitler and Goering and Goebbels, and all those leaders who had brought so much misery upon the world. Then some said it was not true. Back and forth the rumors flew. Country by country, Europe became liberated.

Soon, very soon, our turn would come.

39

Liberation, the War is Over

At 3 p.m. on May 8th, 1945, Winston Churchill, speaking over British radio, declared that peace had come to Europe. The time was known beforehand to those who had radios, and the leaders of the Home Front in Narvik had sent out their last *parole* telling people that as soon as this message of peace had been proclaimed the church bells would start ringing, and the Norwegian flag could be raised to fly free and proud again from our tall flagpoles. One of the three editors of the Narvik underground paper who now came out in the open was my fourth grade teacher, Harry Westrheim. He had been an active member of the Resistance, and even of the very secret XU organization.

We counted the minutes and seconds until 3 p.m. And then they started, those beautiful church bells, both in Narvik and in our old white Ankenes church.

I stood on the front staircase the moment those fast, happy bells started filling our world, and I felt overwhelmed. Tears popped out and made my face wet. I almost gasped for breath. We were free! Was it really true? Was the war over for sure? Yes, it was true. The long, dark winter of war was over. Springtime was here in every way. I remembered what we had sung in the children's choir. Peace would come. Peace had come.

And now the flags flew to tops from three or four houses below us. It seemed to me that they waved like crazy, moved like animals in springtime when they are first let out from their winter stalls. Look at me, look at me, I am free, I am free.

For a whole hour the bells rang. They could not remain silent, and they expressed better than any words how we felt. Then the jubilation began. Wherever we went joy had taken hold of our people. They smiled, shook hands, congratulated each other that peace had come. They hugged and cried. The Norwegian flag went up on every available flag pole. Its bright red rectangles with the white and dark blue cross seemed to belong with the blue sky, the white mountains, the greening foothills, and the gray-blue fjord.

That evening we put burning candles in as many windows as possible. They were candles of peace. We kept them burning all night although we had no darkness in Northern Norway at this time of the year.

In school we sang and sang, all the national songs and hymns, nature songs, patriotic songs. No one could stop us now. We read poems from the national-romantic period in literature, and relished everything that was uniquely Norwegian, uniquely ours. I truly felt that no country in the world was as wonderful as Norway. It was the only one I had known.

The German soldiers stayed inside the barracks and official buildings they had occupied. Norwegian men with armbands with various letters such as HF and *Milorg* showed up everywhere. They were our neighbors and fellow citizens who had been part of the Underground or Resistance Movement. We had heard whispered rumors about some of them, but were surprised that certain others had also belonged. For a few days they were the unofficial authority as the Nazi officials were stripped of their jobs.

Radios came out of hiding. Our King, Håkon the Seventh, spoke on the radio from abroad. He admonished the Norwegian people to act with dignity and reason, not to do anything rash, not to seek to get even with anyone, for he said justice would be meted out in time, in a lawful and orderly manner. He and his family, together with the lawful Norwegian Government, would return to Norway as soon as possible.

At the end of his speech he repeated the motto he had chosen when he was elected Norway's king 40 years earlier; *"Alt for Norge!"* All for Norway! We were so moved. Tears came easily.

The Germans soldiers upstairs packed up and left. Shablashan came down to say goodbye. He was glad the war was over, and hoped he would be able to go home to what used to be Czechoslovakia. He did not know if any of his family was alive. Mama shook hands with him and said, "God be with you!" They both cried.

We were able to go upstairs again. The rooms smelled like a barn, for they had been horse handlers. We opened all the windows. Mama washed the windows and all the woodwork as well as the floor in hot, soapy water. The smell lingered. Later on we had to tear all the wallpaper off, and put up new. Finally the smell went away.

One day as we were sitting down to dinner we saw two Russian prisoners outside our house. They looked in through the window. Papa said we ought to invite them in. They came in and we made room for them around the table. Our dinner that day was codfish tongues in curry sauce and boiled potatoes. Since the Russians were our guests we offered them the serving bowls first. The first one started eating the potatoes right from the bowl. We did not know what to do, but my dad just smiled at him and shook his head. Then he took the bowl and showed him how he was supposed to put a couple of potatoes on his own plate, and pass the bowl to the next person. My brother and I began snickering. We all ended up laughing—the Russians also. We wondered if this was how they did it in Russia, or if five years of being prisoners of war had made them forget how to act civilized.

They spoke only a few words of German, so the conversation around the table was not lively. They wondered what they were eating. We tried to make hand movements showing a fish swimming, then pointed to our tongues. They looked at each other with big eyes, but they ate. There were no leftovers that day.

Soon trains from Sweden brought army trucks and real Norwegian soldiers who had been part of the Allied forces. The trucks made such strange smells. They ran on diesel. The German trucks had used wood chips for fuel.

In the light summer evenings my girlfriends and I walked to Narvik to meet the Norwegian soldiers. I was thirteen and a half, and not into the boy-girl scene yet, but I had begun to feel stirrings of interest in the opposite sex. It was fun talking to these soldiers and I made them laugh a lot. Most of them did not come from Northern Norway.

One of these evenings we became aware of some commotion in the town square. We ran to find out what was going on. People were carrying cans and bags and boxes, as much as their arms could hold. Someone had opened one of the German food storage rooms, and now old and young were helping themselves to anything they could find. I had nothing to carry stuff in so I took off my sweater and made a sort of container out of it. I filled it with canned corned beef and macaroni. Those were the only items left. My girl friends did the same. We walked back to Ankenes again. It was a one-hour walk, but we thought nothing of that. The bundle was heavy, though.

When I came home I proudly displayed my catch. My parents had second thoughts about this. They told me that I had probably broken the law, and must not do that again regardless of what other people did. They were displeased that Norwegian citizens could do this, and were afraid that the war had damaged us in more than one way. We did eat the food, but it did not taste as great as I had anticipated.

Every day we waited and hoped for food supplies to start coming in. We especially wondered when we would get bananas. We had not seen any of those for over five years. Mama said it would probably be many weeks before the boats could get to Norway from so far away.

As the German soldiers were disarmed and sent away, we began to get milk and cheese regularly. We were also able to buy "real" flour which came from Sweden. One day this wonderful smell of bread baking drifted out the windows. We could not wait for the loaves to cool off before we begged a taste. Even though it was still a little warm Mama was able to slice it, and put rhubarb jam on. Real bread! It was worth a celebration. We sat outside in the sunshine, relishing every bite. It was a sign of good times ahead.

Only nine days after liberation came the 17th of May. Big celebrations were due, but the time was short to prepare. Some old musicians got their brass and wind instruments together and formed a small band. Children whose homes had not burned during the war searched and found old Norwegian flags.

The rest of us made our own by coloring flags on white pieces of paper. We knew the proportions: 6-1-2-1-6 on the short side, and 6-1-2-1-12 on the long side (red-white-blue-white-red). We fastened these homemade flags to sticks, and now we were ready.

For the first time in many years the birch trees had turned green this early. Big swags of green were fastened on porches and doorways, and on the platform where the speeches would be given. But for us the biggest event was the children's parade, the first one since 1939. Now we had 1945.

The band led, and we sang, as loud as we could, *"Ja, vi elsker dette landet!"* Yes, we love this very land!

People were standing along the side of the road, or hanging out the windows. Some were watching from their yards or on the steps going in to the house. We walked and sang, waved our flags and shouted hurrah! and sang some more.

On the route we passed a German ship which was still docked down on our side of the harbor. The sailors stood on the deck, looking at us. As I marched past them my young heart swelled with joy and pride. "We made it, we made it," my heart sang.

We made it through—five years of fear and deprivation, hunger and threadbare clothes—five years of having to speak carefully, and not tell secrets we had learned about the Underground or hidden radios—five years of no home or occupied homes—five years of hearing that people we knew had been imprisoned or executed—five years of missing family that had fled to Sweden or England—five years of longing for something called Freedom.

But now Freedom was ours. I was so happy I almost could not sing, but I did:

> *Norske menn I hus og hytte*
> *takk din store Gud.*
> *Landet ville han beskytte*
> *skjønt det mørkt så ut.*
> *Alt hva fedrene har kjempet,*
> *mødrene har grett*
> *har den Herre stille lempet*
> *så vi vant, vi vant vår rett.*
> *har den Herre stille lempet*
> *så vi vant, vi vant vår rett.*

> Norsemen, both in house and cottage
> Thank your mighty God.
> He, our nation has defended
> even through the dark.
> All for which our fathers struggled
> and our mothers wept
> has the Lord in silence brought forth
> thus we won, we won our rights.
> Has the Lord in silence brought forth
> thus we won, we won our rights.

The war was truly over. Grade school was over. Childhood was over. I was becoming a young woman. The future looked bright with peace, and the promise of endless possibilities.

And so I marched on.

Sources

Sverre Steen and Arnold Eskeland, *Norges Krig 1940-1945 Volumes I, II, and III,* Gyldendal Norsk Forlag, Oslo,1950

Nils A. Ytreberg, *Narviks Historie, vol. II,* Merkur Boktrykkeri, Oslo 1954

Magnus Pettersen, *Ofoten III,* Ofoten Bygdeboknemnd, Hvarings Grafiske A/S, Narvik, 1994

Ole F. Berg, *I Skjæjrgården og på Havet,* Bergersens Trykkeri A/S, Oslo 1995

Fremover, Narvik newspaper, May and June, 1990, May 1995

Marie Ostrems dagbok, J.W.Eides Forlag, Bergen 1962

Jens Mostad, *Opplevelser I Krigsaarene 1940-1945,* Merkur Boktrykkeri Nyt A/S, Oslo 1947

Paul G. Vigness, Ph.D., *The German Occupation of Norway,* Vantage Press, N.Y., 1970

Andenaes, Riste, & Skodvin, *Norway And The Second World War,* Aschehoug, 1966

Robert Leckie, *Delivered from Evil: The Saga of W.W.II,* Harper and Row, Publisher, New York, 1987

The Marshall Cavendish Illustrated Encyclopedia of World War II, Vol.II, Marshall Cavendish Corporation, New York, Library of Congress Catalog No 72-95429, Printed in Great Britain

---

Photographs are from the personal collections of Ingebjørg, Aase and Hanna. Hanna also drew the sketches of the *spark* and the Christmas tree decorations.

Hanna Aasvik Helmersen

Hanna Aasvik grew up in Ankenes, Nordland, Norway. After *examen artium,* she went to Denmark for a four-year course in Physical Therapy. She has practiced her profession for 43 years in four countries—Denmark, Norway, Pakistan, and the United States. She is a life member of the American Physical Therapy Association. In 1957 she immigrated to the United States to marry Hjaltar Helmersen, also from Northern Norway, whom she had met some years earlier. They live in a suburb of Seattle, Washington. She earned a Masters of Art degree in Psychology from Seattle University in 1983. Some of her many interests are: music, literature, languages, psychology, religion, gardening, cooking, and healthful living. Hjaltar and Hanna have both been active in the Norwegian community in Seattle. They have two sons and five grandchildren.

Her sister and brother-in-law, Kirsten and Wilhelm Qvigstad also emigrated to the Seattle area, in 1958. Their families have been very close. Hanna has traveled to Europe frequently to visit her other siblings who now live in Norway, Sweden, Denmark and Spain. At a family reunion in 1970, the cousins spoke five different languages.

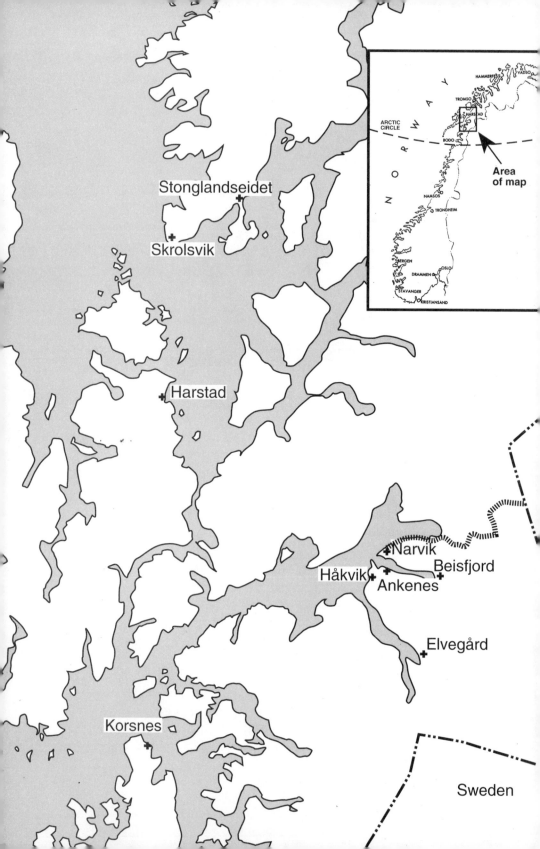

Stonglandseidet

Skrolsvik

Harstad

Narvik
Beisfjord
Håkvik
Ankenes

Elvegård

Korsnes

Sweden

ARCTIC
CIRCLE

N
O
R
W
A
Y

HAMMERFEST
VADSO
TROMSO
HARSTAD
BODO

NAMSOS
TRONDHEIM

BERGEN
DRAMMEN
OSLO
STAVANGER
KRISTIANSAND

Area
of map

Order Form

Katrina Remembers..

...various chapters of her childhood farm life.

by
Jean Clark Kaldahl
Norwegian Dialect Stories

Tell your friends of this fountain of memories and heritage as lived by 10-year-old Katrina, who speaks with a Norwegian brogue. She takes you with her to go after the cows, gather eggs, and take lunch to the threshers...and more with *lutefisk*!!

The paperback illustrated book is in an album with two cassette tapes so you can hear it, too. The cheapest way for you to order is by mail. Below is the price of one book. Contact me first, if you wish numerous books.

Fill out a copy of this order form and mail it to the address below, with a check or money order made out to:

Jean Clark Kaldahl
KALDAHL WRITINGS
P.O. Box 574
Port Townsend, WA 98368-0574

Mail to: Name _____

Street _____

City _____ State _____ Zip _____

Please send me _____ copy(ies) of

Katrina Remembers...

(Prices as of November 1, 2001)

Album: (Book & 2 Tapes) $23.00 each   Total _____

Washington Residents   add 8.2% Sales Tax _____

Packaging and Postage - in the U.S.A. only
Standard Mail or $2.45 each
Priority Mail $4.45 each   Total _____

TOTAL ENCLOSED _____

CONTENTS
Introduction..indentifying Katrina

Order Form

Katrina Remembers..

...various chapters of her childhood farm life.

by
Jean Clark Kaldahl
Norwegian Dialect Stories

Tell your friends of this fountain of memories and heritage as lived by 10-year-old Katrina, who speaks with a Norwegian brogue. She takes you with her to go after the cows, gather eggs, and take lunch to the threshers...and more with *lutefisk*!!

The paperback illustrated book is in an album with two cassette tapes so you can hear it, too. The cheapest way for you to order is by mail. Below is the price of one book. Contact me first, if you wish numerous books.

Fill out a copy of this order form and mail it to the address below, with a check or money order made out to:

Jean Clark Kaldahl
KALDAHL WRITINGS
P.O. Box 574
Port Townsend, WA 98368-0574

Mail to: Name _____

Street _____

City _____ State _____ Zip _____

Please send me _____ copy(ies) of

Katrina Remembers...

(Prices as of November 1, 2001)
Album: (Book & 2 Tapes) $23.00 each   Total _____

Washington Residents   add 8.2% Sales Tax _____

Packaging and Postage - in the U.S.A. only
    Standard Mail or $2.45 each
    Priority Mail $4.45 each   Total _____

TOTAL ENCLOSED _____

CONTENTS

Introduction..indentifying Katrina